What **MAXnotes**® Will Do for You

KU-783-023

This book is intended to help you absorb the essential contents and features of James Joyce's *Dubliners* and to help you gain a thorough understanding of the work. The book has been designed to do this more quickly and effectively than any other study guide.

For best results, this **MAXnotes** book should be used as a companion to the actual work, not instead of it. The interaction between the two will greatly benefit you.

To help you in your studies, this book presents the most up-to-date interpretations of every section of the actual work, followed by questions and fully explained answers that will enable you to analyze the material critically. The questions also will help you to test your understanding of the work and will prepare you for discussions and exams.

Meaningful illustrations are included to further enhance your understanding and enjoyment of the literary work. The illustrations are designed to place you into the mood and spirit of the work's settings.

The **MAXnotes** also include summaries, character lists, explanations of plot, and section-by-section analyses. A biography of the author and discussion of the work's historical context will help you put this literary piece into the proper perspective of what is taking place.

The use of this study guide will save you the hours of preparation time that would ordinarily be required to arrive at a complete grasp of this work of literature. You will be well prepared for classroom discussions, homework, and exams. The guidelines that are included for writing papers and reports on various topics will prepare you for any added work which may be assigned.

The **MAXnotes** will take your grades "to the max."

Dr. Max Fogiel
Program Director

Contents

**Each story includes List of Characters,
Summary, Analysis, Study Questions and
Answers, and Suggested Essay Topics.**

SECTION ONE

Introduction

The Life and Work of James Joyce

James Joyce was born in 1882 in a suburb of Dublin, Ireland in a large, Catholic family, and received a private education in Jesuit schools; thereafter, he attended University College, Dublin, on scholarship. His family life, though warm, was immersed in the turbulent Irish politics of the time and the early arguments Joyce overheard about various Irish leaders filtered their way into Joyce's fiction.

When Joyce was nine, the family's finances began to dwindle when his father was forced into early retirement (never finding steady work again). The family moved several times, each resulting in a less respectable address. With poverty looming, however, Joyce's father arranged for the boys to attend a prestigious Jesuit prep school on scholarship. Despite the boys' promising education, the Joyce's family life was fractious because of financial worries and the father's drinking; James was the only son to have a close relationship with the elder Joyce.

Entering University College, Dublin, on scholarship in 1898, Joyce studied English literature and foreign languages. At university, Joyce began to formulate his feelings towards family, church, and homeland that would be played and replayed in his fiction. Like his hero Stephen Dedalus (who appears in *A Portrait of the Artist as a Young Man* and *Ulysses*), Joyce chose not to remain a member of the Catholic church; nevertheless, he disapproved of religious hypocrisy and retained the benefits of his liberal and intellectual Jesuit training. Unlike Stephen, Joyce had a terrific sense of humor, as much of his fiction and many of his letters make clear.

Even as a youth, he loved puns, word games, titillating malaprop-isms, etc. This fascination makes itself evident in *Portrait*, *Ulysses* and especially *Finnegans Wake*.

Another strong influence on Joyce's work was his love for and ability in music. He studied voice and piano, briefly considering a career as an Irish tenor (he befriended the great John McCormack) as a young man. His earliest collection of poems, *Chamber Music* (1907), is based mostly on ballad form, and music's importance is stressed throughout his work. However, Joyce's increasingly dete-riorating eyesight forced him to rely more on hearing music than seeing it. As a result, accurate representations of sounds, accents, voices, street noises, folksongs, etc., bring color and naturalism to his writing.

In college, Joyce was drawn to study drama, particularly Henrik Ibsen, who was a lifelong influence. After publishing an early ar-ticle on Ibsen in a drama journal in 1900, the 18 year-old critic re-ceived a (translated) note of thanks from the Norwegian dramatist. Recognition from a famous founder of the modern dramatic move-ment enabled Joyce to view himself as a budding European intel-lectual/writer rather than a mere Irish college boy. In effect, it was a turning point in his early artistic life.

Joyce toyed with medical school after college, while simulta-neously trying to establish himself in Dublin literary circles. Mov-ing to Paris in 1902, ostensibly to study medicine, Joyce found there a liberated society completely opposite that of his native city. Joyce felt he could be intellectually freer as an exile in Paris. In fact, the theme of the *exile* appears throughout his fiction and is the title of his play. As Ellmann states, Joyce realized that the trip to Paris tran-scended a faint desire to study medicine or escape from his family's financial misery. "To measure himself and his country," Ellmann states, "he needed to take the measure of a more alien world." (Ellman, *James Joyce*, 110)

For the rest of his life, with the exception of a few intermittent stays in Dublin, Joyce made Trieste, Paris, and Zurich his most fre-quent homes, although his writing always focussed on the Irish capital.

Having moved back to Dublin from Paris in 1903 to comfort his dying mother, Joyce felt stultified in his native city but lacked the means to travel. Occasionally, he worked with ambition, beginning preliminary work that would evolve into *Portrait* in a single day. In 1904, he met his future wife, Nora Barnacle, an unsophisticated country girl from the west coast of Ireland, and was almost instantaneously smitten with her. Though not nearly his equal intellectually, Nora provided the source and inspiration for much of Joyce's ground-breaking portrayals of women in his fiction, most notably for *Ulysses'* Molly Bloom. That same year, the unmarried couple departed for Paris together (a scandalous act at the time) and remained together—despite Joyce's temperament, his extreme jealousy, and numerous financial troubles—for the rest of their lives.

In 1914, the year *Dubliners* finally reached publication, *A Portrait of the Artist as a Young Man* was also published in magazine installments, and published as a novel in 1916. *Portrait* is mainly, though not entirely, autobiographical, taking place (like all of Joyce's work) in Dublin. Using the technique of stream-of-consciousness narration, Joyce attempts to show the evolution of a young artist as he frees himself from the restrictions of religious parochialism and a clinging, suffering family. His hero, Stephen Dedalus, the renegade ex-Catholic, reflects Joyce's own early conflicts between his devotion to art and traditional spiritual duty. Like Stephen, Joyce believed that art was his religion and literature the definitive affirmation of the human spirit.

Stephen Dedalus appears again in Joyce's most famous work, *Ulysses*, the chronicling of the events of a single summer's day in Dublin, 1904. Using the Greek Ulysses myth as a basis for its structure, the novel studies the experience of moment-to-moment events through the eyes of several key characters. Heavily reliant on the stream-of-consciousness method, *Ulysses* also employs the technique of free indirect discourse, in which the author's narrative style mimics the tone and language use of the character perceiving the events described.

Serialized in a Paris journal, *Ulysses*, like *Dubliners*, faced obstacles in publishing because of its sexual content, its publication temporarily halted in France due to obscenity charges. Published finally in French in 1922, the novel was smuggled out of Paris by curious readers and intellectuals for several years before the English edition was finally cleared of obscenity charges in the United States in 1934.

Visiting a family friend in the midst of the obscenity hearings, Joyce was told by his mother that the novel "was not fit to read." If such was the case, Joyce responded, "life isn't fit to live." (Ellmann, *James Joyce*, 537). This clarifies Joyce's stance (shared by D. H. Lawrence, Jean Rhys, Gertrude Stein, Djuna Barnes, among others) that literature was an appropriate arena for discussions about and explorations of sexual issues. Joyce believed that *Ulysses* reflected real life among working-class Dubliners; all aspects of such life were worthy of examination.

Over the course of many years and despite many costly operations, Joyce's eyesight, always weak, grew increasingly worse. The editing process of *Ulysses* (first in French, then in English) was grueling for him, and as he began writing his last major work, *Finnegans Wake*, his eyesight was almost completely lost. The prose poem, begun in 1923, has been described as a "labyrinth" of literary devices and complex, sometimes arcane, references. Though Joyce considered it his masterwork and its difficulty has made it a challenge to Joyce scholars, it remains less accessible to most readers, who are only somewhat familiar with it.

While Joyce's literary achievements and obsessive devotion to his art have made him a pillar of Modernist literature, they also made life difficult for himself and his family. He secured a loyal English patron to subsidize his writing, but—in light of his lifelong inability to manage money—his wife and two children rarely enjoyed the material comforts of his success. Although his work earned him admirers throughout the world, Joyce's sense of suspicion and imperious ego often alienated supporters when he needed them most. In addition, his terrible eyesight made writing and editing, the mainstays of his life, agony.

When *Finnegan's Wake* was finally published in 1939, Joyce's health was failing and his daughter, having suffered a severe nervous breakdown, was confined to a Swiss institution. While *Finnegan's Wake* failed to receive the reception that Joyce felt it deserved, his reputation among the writers of the period was certain. When France fell to the Nazis in 1940, James and Nora left Paris for neutral Switzerland, where Joyce died in 1941.

Historical Background

As he portrays it in his work, Joyce's Dublin was composed mostly of lower-to middle-class residents oppressed by financial hardships, foreign political dominance, fractiousness among rival Irish nationalist groups, and the overwhelming influence of the Irish Catholic Church. Combined, in Joyce's eyes, these forces and travails left the ordinary Dubliner with few options for self-expression or freedom of the soul; hence, Joyce's theme of "paralysis" was established.

In the late 1800s, Ireland was still reeling from the agricultural disasters of mid-century and the massive Irish immigration (mainly to the United States) that followed. Several references in the stories suggest that well-paying employment was scarce and that even working class Dubliners struggled under subsistence wages. Consistently throughout the stories, characters agonize over a crown or even a shilling; this underscores the prevailing financial difficulties among most citizens.

Politically, Ireland was ruled by the British monarchy, and the attitude among the Irish towards the occupying British ranged from one of skepticism and distrust to open hostility. In addition to its aversion to Catholicism, the British government disdained the Irish for their general lack of education (especially in the countryside), their superstitious ways, and the often squalid living conditions necessitated by the country's weak economy. That the British profited from its presence in Ireland—even while regarding its people with contempt—only served to further infuriate the Irish at the British presence.

During the 1880s, the possibility for Ireland's sovereignty was strengthened by the efforts of political leader Charles Stewart Parnell. Owing to his influence, political savvy and uncompromising support of home rule, Ireland's independence seemed more viable under Parnell's leadership than ever before. However, the disclosure of a romantic scandal in 1889 sullied Parnell's reputation, allowing his opponents and groups of zealous Catholics (Parnell was Protestant), working in concert, to discredit him and weaken his power base. This turnaround in fate and the betrayal of even his closest allies broke Parnell, leading to his political defeat and—ultimately—his death in 1891.

Turn-of-the-century Dublin, as portrayed in Joyce's collection, is still haunted by Parnell's ghost and the promise of Irish independence that died with him. Gradually, many Irish realized they had themselves to blame for allowing Parnell's dream of independence to vanish, and the themes of failed promise and betrayal are common in the works of many Irish writers of the period, Joyce's especially.

Finally, an overwhelming force in the Ireland of Joyce's period was that of the Irish Catholic Church, since a vast majority of the Irish were Catholics. According to his biographer, Richard Ellmann, Joyce believed that the "real sovereign of Ireland [was] the Pope" (Ellmann, *James Joyce*, 256). Although Joyce left the Church, Ellmann adds, he "continued to denounce all his life the deviousness of Papal policy," finding the Church and the papacy "deaf" to Irish cries for help (Ellmann, *James Joyce*, 257). Clearly, Joyce believed the Church reacted inadequately in failing to help unburden the Irish of the hostile British presence, nor did it sufficiently attempt to lift Ireland out of its literal and figurative poverty. He believed Church doctrine encouraged docility and subservience on the part of the Irish, this attitude only further enhancing Ireland's political exploitation and lack of independence.

In preparation for *Dubliners*, Joyce kept a notebook of revelations, or "epiphanies," which are central to understanding the stories. While the word most commonly describes a religious revelation, Joyce's understanding of the epiphany is the recognition of the essential essence of a moment, an exchange, an experience. It is the sudden "revelation of the whatness of a thing," Joyce maintained, and in *Dubliners*, the epiphany marks a character's realization about him or herself—even if the psychic realization is a painful one. (Ellmann, *James Joyce*, 83).

Joyce composed the *Dubliners* stories with great ease, basing groups of stories on his experiences in childhood, adolescence, and mature life. In a letter to his brother Stanislaus in 1905, Joyce stated Dublin's importance as a world capital and indicated his desire to present it to the world (Ellmann, *James Joyce*, 208). Though he lived abroad while writing about his homeland, Joyce did not allow his portrayal of Dublin to be cosmetized by a sense of homesickness. In a speech he characterized Ireland as a country "weakened by centuries of useless struggle and broken treaties," where "individual initiative is paralyzed[.]" (Ellmann, *James Joyce*, 258).

Not surprisingly, publishers backed away from his unblinking portrait of Dublin's citizenry; it took Joyce an exhausting nine years to see *Dubliners* published. "I seriously believe," Joyce wrote to would-be publisher Grant Richards in 1905, "that you will retard the course of civilisation in Ireland by preventing the Irish people from having one good look at themselves in my nicely polished looking glass" (Ellmann, *Selected Letters*, 90). Although Richards appreciated the collection and even signed a contract, his printer objected to the profanity and tawdry scenes included in therein. When these were brought to Richards' attention, he asked Joyce to remove them, but the stubborn Joyce refused and Richards cancelled his commitment. *Dubliners* travelled from publisher to publisher, each one disturbed at the stories' pessimism, sordid scenes, profanity and sexual subtleties. The image Joyce reflected was far from complimentary, but he remained convinced that it was accurate and therapeutic. *Dubliners* portrays the soul of that city, chronicling the decay of its morals and the weakening of its spiritual life by focussing on the psychic and emotional paralysis of its inhabitants.

When finally published in 1914, sales of *Dubliners* were disappointing. While intellectuals such as W. B. Yeats and Ezra Pound appreciated *Dubliners*, most critics' objections were similar to those of the many unwilling publishers: they found the stories depressing, showing only an unseemly side of Dublin. Further, they had difficulty finding the "point" in the collection, failing to realize that to read *Dubliners* (indeed, all of Joyce's work) one must read for symbolical meaning.

As Joyce's subsequent literary works became more well-known, critics began to develop the skills of symbolic reading required to appreciate the *Dubliners* stories.

Master List of Characters
The Sisters

Narrator—*Boy, 8–9 years old.*

Father Flynn (dead)—*Boy's mentor.*

Narrator's Aunt and Uncle

Nannie and Eliza—*Priest's elderly sisters.*

Old Cotter—*Family friend.*

An Encounter

Narrator—*Boy, 8–9 years old.*

Mahoney—*School friend of the Narrator.*

Leo Dillon—*School firend of the Narrator.*

Joe Dillon—*Leo's brother.*

Older Man in Field—*Quite likely a sexual pervert.*

Araby

Narrator—*Boy, 9–12 years old.*

Mangan's sister—*Sister of narrator's friend with whom the boy is in love.*

Narrator's Aunt and Uncle

Eveline

Eveline Hill—*Young woman, 18–20 years old.*

Eveline's Alcoholic Father

Eveline's Mother—*Who died and Eveline loved.*

Frank—*Eveline's betrothed.*

After the Race

Jimmy Doyle—*Wealthy 20–21 year-old Irishman.*

Charles Segouin—*Owner of a French race car, his friend.*

Andre Riviere—*Friend of Segouin.*

Villona—*Hungarian friend of Segouin.*

Routh—*English friend of Segouin.*

Farley—*American friend of Riviere.*

Two Gallants

Corley—*A womanizer about 25 years old.*

Lenehan—*His buddy, approximately the same age.*

Servant Girl ("Slavey")—*Whom Corley is dating.*

The Boarding House

Mrs. Mooney—*Owner of the boarding house.*

Polly Mooney—*Her 19-year-old daughter.*

Bob Doran—*Boarder with whom Polly has become romantically involved.*

A Little Cloud

Little Chandler—*Thirty-ish clerk and amateur poet.*

Ignatius Gallaher—*Little Chandler's school friend, now a journalist living in London.*

Little's Wife (Annie) and Baby Son

Counterparts

Farrington—*Forty-ish clerk and alcoholic.*

Mr. Alleyne—*Farrington's boss.*

Weathers—*An English entertainer whom Farrington meets in a pub.*

Several of Farrington's Drinking Companions

Clay

Maria—*Middle-aged worker in an Irish charitable laundry.*

Joe Donnelly—*Her nephew.*

Joe's Family

A Painful Case

James Duffy—*Middle-aged ascetic and scholar.*

Emily Sinico—*Middle-aged married woman who becomes attached to Duffy intellectually and personally.*

Ivy Day in the Committee Room

Old Jack—*Caretaker of headquarters.*

O'Connor—*Young political canvasser.*

Hynes—*Canvasser whom others suspect of working for the rival side.*

Henchy—*A canvasser.*

Crofton—*A canvasser.*

Lyons—*A canvasser.*

Richard Tierney (not present)—*Politician running for office in the Royal Exchange Ward and for whom the canvassers are working.*

Father Keon—*De-frocked priest and friend of Tierney.*

Charles Stewart Parnell—*(dead) Irish Revolutionary in whose honor ivy is worn on the lapel to commemorate anniversary of his death.*

A Mother

Mrs. Kearney—*Overbearing mother and socially ambitious member of Dublin middle class.*

Mr. Kearney—*Her quiet, ineffectual husband.*

Kathleen Kearney—*Her teenage daughter.*

Mr. Holohan—*Assistant secretary to the* Eire Abu *Society.*

Mr. Fitzpatrick—*Secretary to the* Eire Abu *Society.*

Grace

Tom Kernan—*A tea merchant and alcoholic.*

Messrs. Power, Cunningham, M'Coy and Fogarty—*Tom Kernan's friends.*

Mrs. Kernan—*His wife.*

Father Purdon—*Priest running the "businessman's retreat" at the local church.*

The Dead

Gabriel Conroy—*Teacher and amateur writer.*

Gretta Conroy—*His wife.*

Julia and Kate Morkan—*Gabriel's aging aunts, piano and voice teachers in Dublin.*

Mary Jane—*Gabriel's cousin, an unmarried piano teacher who lives with the aunts.*

Molly Ivors—*Gabriel's colleague and passionate Irish nationalist various party guests of the Morkans.*

Michael Furey—*(dead) Adolescent love of Gretta Conroy.*

Summary of the Short Stories

In turn-of-the-century Dublin, the lives of several lower and middle-class Irishmen are described by the author. The first of these stories, "The Sisters," portrays a boy of 8-9 years whose friend and mentor, Father Flynn, has just died. The boy and his aunt pay their respects to Flynn and his sisters at the sisters' house.

In "An Encounter," the narrator and his school-boy friend, Mahoney, cut a day's school to have an adventure in Dublin. Just when it seems that nothing exciting will happen to them, they meet an elderly eccentric in a park. As it turns out, the older man is a sexual pervert and describes to the narrator his fantasies, which frightens the boy.

In "Araby," the narrator describes in retrospect an intense crush he had on a friend's sister when he was about 12-13 years old. At the time, he promised the sister that he'd go to a local fair and bring her back a gift (perhaps making her his girlfriend), but the mission ended with disappointment when he found nothing suitable for her.

"Eveline" finds a 19-year-old girl about to leave her father's home in Dublin to elope to South America with her beau. However, she is too afraid of change and believes she owes her loyalty to her father; at the story's end, she won't join her pleading boyfriend on the trans-atlantic steamer.

Jimmy Doyle, in "After the Race," is one of the collection's few well-to-do characters. Having invested a large sum of money in a

French racecar, he joins his French friends in a cross-Dublin auto race and meets with them later in the evening for dinner and gambling. However, he plays poorly and losses an untold (but considerable) amount of money at cards.

Corley and Lenehan in "Two Gallants" discuss Corley's latest female conquest and the lengths she'll go to please her boyfriend. By the end of the story, we see that she will even steal money from her employer for Corley, a fact that Lenehan regards with admiration and awe.

Polly Mooney, in "The Boarding House," has ensnared Bob Doran into becoming engaged to her through her seductive behavior and the actions of her calculating and manipulative mother. Doran is helpless against these two conniving women and agrees under force to the marriage although he doesn't feel love for Polly.

"A Little Cloud" describes the fading literary desires of Little Chandler who meets a much more successful friend (a journalist) in a bar after work. At first Little hopes his friend can help his career, but he soon realizes that the man would never help him. Returning home from the pub, Little is extremely discouraged with his life's circumstances.

In "Counterparts," the alcoholic clerk, Farrington, has an argument with his boss and recovers from the fight by getting drunk in a bar after work. At the bar, surrounded by his cronies, he's humiliated by a fellow patron and returns home so angry and frustrated that he beats his young son.

Maria, in "Clay," visits her brother and his family on Hallowe'en, bringing them cakes and goodies. Although they're happy to see her, a series of minor upsets discompose Maria, and it's difficult for her to enjoy herself at this much-anticipated party.

James Duffy, in "A Painful Case," meets a woman at a concert with whom he becomes close friends. When their relationship becomes too intense for him, he breaks it off, only to discover several years later that the woman has committed suicide on a railway in the city. Though he initially blames the woman's unbalanced mental state for this occurrence, he comes to realize the part he's played in her death.

A group of political workers in "Ivy Day in the Committee Room" gather together at party headquarters to drink stout, complain about corrupt Dublin politics and reminisce about the happier times when Charles Stewart Parnell was still active in Irish politics. One member of the group recites a poem he wrote to commemorate the death of Parnell.

Mrs. Kearney in "A Mother" is an overbearing stage parent who wants her daughter Kathleen to play the piano at an Irish concert and be paid the contracted fee for the performance. When the directors of the pageant try to unfairly nullify Kathleen's contract, Mrs. Kearney becomes furious, barring her daughter from performing further and threatening the management of the concert. Neither side can compromise enough to reach an agreement.

In "Grace," three of Tom Kernan's friends and drinking buddies convince him to attend a religious retreat with them in order to clean up their lives and atone for their sins. Although it's unlikely that any of them understand the significance of their actions, they attend the retreat together, convinced that this experience will help save their souls.

Finally, Gabriel Conroy and his wife Gretta, in "The Dead," attend the Christmas party of Gabriel's aging aunts. Throughout the evening Gabriel constantly second-guesses his actions and never truly relaxes or enjoys himself. After the party, as he's about to approach his wife romantically, Gabriel learns from her that, as a teenager, she was deeply in love with a country boy who died of heartbreak over her. This news so upsets the unsuspecting Gabriel that it shatters his picture of his life, forcing him to reconsider everything he's previously taken for granted.

Estimated Reading Time

Although all are fairly short, most of the stories in *Dubliners* are deep, and some of the vocabulary is complex. Therefore, set aside at least a week (ideally, two weeks), with several sittings, to read *Dubliners*. It is suggested that each story be read through once, while underlining unfamiliar words and marking items of importance. After looking up the vocabulary in a dictionary, and reviewing the commentary and notes, re-read the story; many more things will be noticed the second time and the reading will be even more enjoyable.

Notice, too, that these stories are meant to fit together: the theme in one often relates to that in several others, and many characters have similar (although never identical) circumstances. Consider the people of *Dubliners* as a group and try to understand their struggles and disappointments. Joyce intended to show his city to itself and the world, and these stories will recreate the atmosphere of that period in Dublin if they are read attentively.

Dubliners

The Sisters

New Characters:

Narrator: *boy, 8–9 years old*

Father Flynn (dead): *boy's mentor*

Narrator's Aunt and Uncle

Nannie and Eliza: *priest's elderly sisters*

Old Cotter: *family friend*

Summary

This story is narrated by a young boy, probably about eight or nine, discussing the imminent death of Father Flynn, an older priest whom he has befriended. After three strokes, the priest is paralyzed, but the boy hesitates to ask for certain if he has died. His aunt, uncle, and a family friend discuss the priest's odd habits, the friend adding that the priest might not be a good influence on a younger person. The boy takes offense at what he believes is a patronizing statement, but says nothing.

After having a nightmare about Fr. Flynn, the boy discovers a notice at the priest's sisters' home that Flynn has died. Rather than feeling mournful, however, the boy feels an inexplicable freedom. He recollects the details about Catholicism that he learned from Flynn, but he still cannot interpret his giddiness.

Going to pay his respects with his aunt later in the evening, the boy is distracted, cannot pray, and cannot make smalltalk with Eliza (one of Fr. Flynn's sisters) as his aunt can. Instead he listens to the sisters and his aunt discuss the priest's disappointing career and life in the clergy, which was muddled by his dropping a chalice during a mass earlier in his career. Eliza claims that this error—coupled with the heavy demands of the priesthood—began to wear down his peace of mind, even implying that Fr. Flynn had begun to lose his mind. The boy, still contemplating the priest and their relationship, says nothing.

Analysis

Father Flynn, the dying priest in "The Sisters," has suffered three strokes and now lies paralyzed on the brink of death. This paralysis is the watchword for Joyce's entire collection of stories, as virtually all the significant characters in *Dubliners* are psychically paralyzed by their life circumstances. Young and old, they are inert or helpless in the face of their own suffering and indecision. The narrator of this story, a young boy who has befriended Flynn, recognizes the fearsome quality of the paralysis and also longs to understand it, "to be nearer to it and to look upon its deadly work."

Although the boy is seen by his aunt as having a "great" friendship with the priest, his family's friend, Old Cotter, perceives something unseemly, believing that Flynn's attention has somehow suffocated—perhaps even corrupted—the boy. The narrator bristles at Cotter's patronizing observations, but the relationship is not, in fact, a healthy one. The boy dreams of Flynn's "grey face," imagining "that it desired to confess something." Both the boy and the face smile "feebly" at each other in the dream, demonstrating an uncertain understanding, even a forgiveness, of the other.

That the priest should show a desire to confess to the boy demonstrates for the reader the perversity of their relationship, as it controverts the priest's main spiritual role. Studying their friendship, we see that the priest "amused himself" during the boy's visits "by putting difficult questions" to him. Flynn forced the narrator into interrogation sessions about minutiae involving church doctrine, requiring him to strain for an answer about spiritual issues which the boy had "always regarded as the simplest acts." In turning the simple and spiritual into the tortuous and strained, Flynn acts as a sadist, with the boy as his compliant victim.

His perversity is further underscored by Joyce's revolting visual description of him: inert and grey, covered with snuff stains and trembling. The narrator's recollection of the priest's smile— his tongue lasciviously lying along his lower lip—"made me feel uneasy in the beginning." It makes the reader uneasy as well, since the sexual image is completely inappropriate. The allusion to sexual impropriety is enhanced slightly further in the boy's dream, which takes place "in some land where the customs were strange—in Persia, I thought..." Though Joyce doesn't complete the dream, the strangeness of the priest's behavior, combined with Old Cotter's admonitions, suggest to the reader the unhealthiness of the bond.

When the narrator learns of Flynn's death, he feels at odds with himself. Knowing he should feel grief, he instead discovers in himself "a sense of freedom as if I had been freed from something by his death." Indeed, the boy has been freed from the priest's oppressive emotional lock on him. Clearly, Flynn represents, as Edward Brandabur has pointed out, "the corrupt features of Irish Catholicism," turning spirituality into a burden and torture (335). In Joyce's mind, Irish Catholicism had leeched life out of the population as the priest had leeched it from the boy. The Irish, Joyce felt, were paralyzed by the trivialities and rules of the Catholic church, as the narrator felt his own coming paralysis in a relationship with the priest.

When he and his aunt visit the dead priest's home to pay their respects, the boy cannot pray beside the coffin as the others do, distracted by thoughts of Flynn and feeling—with his passing— the loss of his own spirituality, albeit a somewhat confused one. Significantly, Flynn holds a chalice (the holy cup used to hold the eucharist) loosely in his hands, symbolizing his insecure grasp on spirituality and his failure as a priest.

Eliza offers the visitors sherry and crackers, symbolic of the wine and wafer during the mass, but the boy refuses them. Partly, this shows his awkwardness with the traditions of the church, though it's not clear that he's abandoned the church altogether. Brandabur suggests that it represents his unwillingness to accept secular substitutes for the sacraments from the secular bearer,

Eliza, as opposed to receiving them from a priest (337). In effect, the boy's refusal is a last vestige of allegiance to the dead priest, regardless of Flynn's suitability for his role.

As Eliza and his aunt discuss Flynn's troubles in the priesthood, it becomes clear that he never thoroughly embraced the spiritual nature of his calling, that he was, in fact, doomed to failure early on. His sister believes his life was "crossed," Joyce's play on words to connect the ill-fated priest to the holy crucifix. The chalice he broke, she adds, "contained nothing," but this too emphasizes Flynn's empty spirituality and the emptiness of Irish Catholicism as a whole. When Flynn was discovered alone and laughing in his confessional, it symbolizes not only his incompetency as a priest but the absurdity he sensed in his inability to function as one. Eliza's comment that there was "something gone wrong" with her brother can include the lives of many Dubliners in the book that this story introduces. In each, the reader finds characters whose souls are paralyzed and who live a contorted and frustrated life similar to that of Father Flynn's.

Study Questions

1. Interpret the significance of the first sentence.

2. When the boy dreams of Fr. Flynn, why does he "try to think of Christmas"?

3. The boy, considering the intricacies of Church doctrine, thinks: "I wondered how anybody had ever found the courage to undertake [learning] them." Explain the irony in this.

4. When viewing the body, the boy says that the candles looked like "pale thin flames." What is the symbolism of this?

5. When Flynn was paralyzed, he dropped his breviary to the floor. Can you interpret this?

6. When Eliza reminisces about her brother, she says that when he was ill, "You wouldn't hear him in the house any more than now." Why is this ironic?

7. Eliza blames the Flynn's dropping of the chalice on the [altar] boy. How does this relate to the narrator?

8. According to his sister, Flynn had dreamed of renting "one of them new-fangled carriages" and riding around for the day, but never did. Is there significance in this?

9. What is the significance of the "idle chalice" on the priest's chest?

10. After viewing the body, the boy doesn't take any refreshment, nor does he talk about the priest. What does this signify?

Answers

1. "No hope" is the theme of the Dubliners' lives. The "third" stroke indicates both the holy trinity and the three times that Christ was betrayed by Peter.

2. He thinks of Christmas because it has an overtly Christian message which he can grasp, unlike the enigmatic approach to the Church that Fr. Flynn represents.

3. Father Flynn never had courage and was actually spiritually bankrupt. The boy admires him for something he doesn't have.

4. Fr. Flynn was a degenerate priest; the flames are an allusion to hellfire.

5. Once Flynn became emotionally paralyzed, he lost his spiritual belief. Therefore, the dropping of the prayer book is a metaphor for the dropping of religion from his life.

6. The irony is this: he was no more alive before his death than he is now that he's passed away.

7. If Flynn blames his failure on the priesthood on this initial incident, he may associate the narrator with the altar boy who allegedly failed him long ago.

8. Evidently, Flynn longed for movement or development, as opposed to the literal and figurative paralysis he had to endure.

9. The chalice (the holy cup) the priest holds is idle; it does nothing and fulfills nothing, just like Fr. Flynn himself.

10. The priest is associated with spiritual as well as physical paralysis. The boy, influenced by having viewed the dead priest, is unable to respond, just as he was.

Suggested Essay Topics

1. Discuss the concept of paralysis as it relates to as many characters in the story as applicable.

2. The boy says that the word "paralysis"…"filled me with fear, and yet I longed to be nearer to it and to look upon its deadly work." If the boy fears the concept of paralysis, how do you interpret his fascination with it?

An Encounter

New Characters:

Narrator: *boy, 8–9 years old*

Mahoney: *school friend of the narrator*

Leo Dillon: *school friend of the narrator*

Joe Dillon: *Leo's brother*

Older Man in Field: *quite likely a sexual pervert*

Summary

The narrator of this story is once again a boy around eight or nine years old (possibly the same boy as in the previous story, but not specified), who loves reading stories of the Wild West and American detective tales. Although he acts out some of these western adventures with his friends, he feels stifled by both these childish games and school. With his two friends, Leo Dillon and Mahoney, the narrator plans to skip school for one day and have a real adventure in Dublin. Each puts in a sixpence to fund the adventure and they agree to meet in the morning.

When Leo Dillon fails to show up (presumably out of cowardice), Mahoney decides that he has forfeited his sixpence and the two split the extra money. They wander the quays and buy snacks, but the boys feel vaguely dissatisfied with their escapade. As the time for their return home draws nearer, they sit aimlessly in a field while Mahoney tries to slingshot a cat.

An older, dishevelled-looking man approaches them and begins to make conversation, asking them about school, books, and girlfriends. Though bored, they respond politely, but the narrator is made uneasy by the man, while Mahoney more or less disregards him. After the conversation turns back to school children, the older man excuses himself and retreats to the edge of the field where Mahoney spots him either urinating or masturbating (written in 1905, the story would not have been published if the act had been more carefully described). Mahoney sees him in the act, but the narrator doesn't look up, even when Mahoney speaks out in alarm. The narrator then suggests that if the older man asks their names, they give him aliases.

After he returns to the narrator, the older man speaks even more animatedly about boys and their proper punishments, and the narrator makes up his mind to leave. Calling out to his friend (using the alias), the narrator is greatly relieved when the friend responds, even though he admits to the reader that he's never liked Mahoney very much.

Analysis

The narrator of this story, possibly the same narrator as in the previous story, seeks a life of adventure and fulfillment; he looks westward, at the Wild West, realizing that "real adventures do not happen to those who remain at home." James Joyce realized this in his own life and fled Ireland, but the narrator—too young to flee—seeks adventure through the imagination and through literature, which "opened doors of escape" from his dreary schoolboy life. Still, detective stories and westerns can't sate his desire for experience, and he longs for an event that goes beyond play-acting and stories.

Stanislaus Joyce writes in his memoir that his brother based this story loosely on a day in their youth when the boys skipped school and met an elderly eccentric in their wanderings (62). However, the story resonates far beyond a day's "miching." The suggestion of perversion, following on the previous story, darkens the

theme of "The Sisters" and augments the vulnerability of this story's narrator.

The other key theme in "An Encounter" is that of deception and betrayal, which pervades virtually every element in the story and many others throughout *Dubliners*.

In order to experience "real adventure," the narrator, Leo Dillon, and Mahoney must deceive the school as well as their families. To secure the plot, the boys each pledge a sixpence; Leo Dillon, however, is too nervous to follow through with the plot and therefore forfeits his money. The narrator sees the forfeiture as somehow unfair to their friend, but Mahoney justifies it without troubling his conscience. Earlier, the narrator comments that "the confused puffy face awakened one of my consciences." Again, the specter of Leo Dillon troubles the narrator—he knows the act is unfair—but he's persuaded to overlook his own instinct by his more ruthless companion.

Most of the boys' actions in the story are predictable: a visit to the quays to look at ships signifies their desire to see the world, to escape. They buy a snack and wander, but the narrator comments twice on how tired they are; the two are worn out by the futility of their quest for adventure. It's obvious to them (and the reader) that their goals were unrealistic, and Mahoney looks ruefully at his slingshot (the closest thing to conquest that either of them can muster).

Ironically, just as they abandon the likelihood for excitement, something unusual does happen to them when approached by the elderly gentleman. At first, his conversation seems banal; Mahoney is more interested in his slingshot than wary of the man. The narrator examines him more closely, though, noticing the "great gaps in his mouth between his yellow teeth." This may remind the reader of Joyce's description of Father Flynn, or just indicate that the man has an unsavory element to him. The narrator also feels an unease with "the words in his mouth," though most of his conversation seems harmless, even meaningless.

Like his demeanor, the man's conversation is also innocuous at first, discussing happy school days. His comments on Edward Bulwer-Lytton, a nineteenth century romantic writer, causes the narrator to scrutinize him further, since some of the author's writings were considered risque in Victorian society. Once again, however, Mahoney fails to see the signs and the narrator doesn't communicate his thoughts to him.

As the older man's conversation progresses, the intensity of his thoughts about school children increases, discussing the soft skin and hair of young girls, repeating his phrases over and over, "surrounding them with his monotonous voice." The narrator hears something alarming in the man's tone, noticing that he spoke "mysteriously as if he were telling us something secret which he did not wish others to overhear." As in the first story, the man makes a confession to the boy, almost seeking approval for his words. This, too, is a perversion, since children customarily seek approval from adults.

When Mahoney notices the man after he briefly excuses himself, it's unclear whether the latter is urinating or masturbating. In 1905, Joyce could never have indicated or specified either act, but Mahoney labels him correctly: "He's a queer old josser!"

The extent of the older man's perversions becomes most clear immediately after this act, when he speaks heatedly about the "nice warm whipping" that some boys deserve, indicating that "there was nothing in the world he would like so well" as to administer such a punishment. In listening, the narrator acts as a kind of collaborator and confessor, since his willingness to listen makes the speaker believe that he might gain understanding from him. In this, the narrator betrays not only his instincts—which tell him to flee—but the man as well, since the boy cannot and does not understand the man's depraved need.

Sensing danger, the boy rises, feigning politeness, and with embarrassment calls out to Mahoney with the alias he'd previously arranged for this situation. Although he feels silly for this "paltry stratagem," the boy is enormously relieved when Mahoney runs toward him, as if to his rescue. To the reader, though, the narrator admits his feelings of guilt, since he actually despises Mahoney for his rude and somewhat violent behavior. This represents the story's final act of betrayal as their adventure draws to a close.

Study Questions

1. Why is it surprising that Joe Dillon chooses the priesthood for a vocation?

2. What is the overall significance of the statement: "Real adventures, I reflected, do not happen to people who remain at home: they must be sought abroad"?

3. Explain how Leo Dillon represents the narrator's conscience.

4. What is the symbolism of the color green in the story?

5. Why does Mahoney brag about having "totties"?

6. Why is Mahoney unconcerned about the bizarre qualities of the man, while the narrator notices them?

7. Why does the old man "seem to plead" with the boy "that [he] should understand him"?

8. What is the significance of Mahoney chasing the cat with a slingshot, and his focus on this?

9. Why does the narrator believe that the older man is repeating his statements about girls as if "he had learned them by heart"?

10. Why does the narrator listen to the older man's warped dialog for so long before leaving?

Answers

1. Because he "played too fiercely" for the other children and is the most violent of the narrator's acquaintances.

2. This concept permeates the lives of many of the Dubliners in this collection: Eveline, Little Chandler, Jimmy Doyle.

3. His "confused puffy face" awakens the narrator's conscience at school; also, Leo chooses not to skip school because he's afraid of the consequences.

4. The boy looks for a green-eyed sailor because green eyes traditionally indicated gullibility. The old gentleman has green eyes but, ironically, it's the boy who seems gullible.

5. He wants to appear grown up. Also, Mahoney is considerably coarser than the narrator, and this off-hand remark indicates this.

6. The narrator is much more observant and deeper than Mahoney.

7. The older man realizes that he's perverted and is hoping for the boy to somehow forgive him in a quasi-religious sense.

8. Mahoney, also, is sadistic, in that he wants to torture/punish a (harmless) cat.

9. The older man seems much more interested in boys than in girls, but it's socially more acceptable for a man to praise the softness of girls' hands, etc. Therefore, he's repeating what's generally accepted.

10. He waits, partly, because he's afraid. Also, he's playing the role of the masochist to the man's sadistic stance, much like the boy and the priest in the previous story.

Suggested Essay Topics

1. The narrator says that Leo Dillon's pudgy face "awakened one of my consciences." How do you interpret the fact that he has more than one conscience?

2. In what ways are the situations of this narrator and the narrator in "The Sisters" similar? In what ways are they different?

Araby

New Characters:

Narrator: *boy, 9–12 years old*

Mangan's sister: *sister of narrator's friend with whom the boy is in love*

Narrator's Aunt and Uncle

Summary

"Araby" is a puzzling story upon first reading because very little happens in terms of plot. The narrator, looking back upon his youth (he is approximately 12 years old), recalls a time when he was

deeply in love with his neighbor, Mangan's sister. Although we never learn the narrator's or the sister's name, we understand that the boy has a vivid imagination and is desperate to prove his devotion to the object of his affection.

When he hears of an exotic neighborhood fair called Araby, the boy asks the sister if she plans to attend. She tells him she must attend a religious retreat instead, and he promises to bring her something as a memento. After he promises her this, the boy is simultaneously excited and terrified at having made this vow, and what his commitment implies.

On the day of Araby, the boy is extremely anxious and cannot concentrate; he fears that his uncle will forget to give him pocket money, and his fears are justified. When the uncle returns home late in the evening, there is a danger that the boy won't be allowed to attend, but his aunt intervenes for him, and he takes a late train to the fair site.

Entering Araby, the boy feels unsettled because it is nearly empty and quite dark. Momentarily, he is so confused that he forgets his mission entirely and must re-focus upon his quest. Upon finding a gift counter with presents suitable for Mangan's sister, the boy loses interest in the knickknacks and declines help from an English shopgirl who offers to serve him. After she looks over at him a few more times (presumably to keep him from stealing), the boy, completely disappointed, walks out, having abandoned his quest and regretting the plans and promise he made.

Analysis

The narrator of "Araby" is obviously telling us a story of his youth from the perspective of adulthood; the sophistication of his language indicates this. Because the boy in the story is still young enough to depend on his aunt and uncle for money, but old enough to fall in love, it's safe to judge his age at about 12–13.

North Richmond Street, where the boy lives (and where the Joyce family also lived) is described as being "blind," or a dead end, but this is only one of the many metaphors and similes which Joyce has worked into his story. The street—like the narrator—is blind to its own limitations, the houses gazing out with "brown imperturbable faces."

The boy's environment tells us much about him. He lives in the former home of a dead priest; in other words, where religion once was, it is no longer. The priest's belongings, especially his books, are further symbols. Scott's *The Abbot* is a romantic novel about Mary I, a Catholic queen of Scotland, while *The Devout Communicant* is, surprisingly, a Protestant book of religious devotion. Finally, *The Memoirs of Vidocq* (the boy's favorite) is a lurid, tell-all confessional by a notorious detective and archcriminal. That these books are the boy's connection to the priest is ironic and revealing.

When the narrator widens the scene to describe his neighborhood, it is "sombre," with "feeble lanterns," "dark muddy lanes" and "odorous" stables and ashpits. The environment is gloomy and oppressive; the only source of light—or uplift—is the object of the boy's love, Mangan's sister. (Note that none of the story's key characters is given a name.)

The sister, described in detail twice in the story, is a figure of light: she stands "defined by the light" of her front door, the lamp light falling on her hair, on "the white curve of her neck," on her hand and petticoat. Like an angel or the Virgin Mary in a vision, the sister appears in an aura of light, complete with a halo. Although the boy behaves toward her as would any adolescent, she is clearly a figure of fervent, almost religious, devotion, and her effect on him is intense: "her name was like a summons to all my foolish blood."

All connections the boy makes to the sister have religious associations. In the noisy and vibrating marketplace, the narrator imagines he carries a "chalice" (the holy cup used during Catholic mass) of love, and her name calls to mind "prayers and praises." His is a "confused adoration" because he has replaced religious love (taught at home and in school) with the earthly love for the young girl. ("Adoration" is a word usually used to describe a love of Christ; clearly, he is confused!) Mangan's sister is the boy's secular angel; thoughts of her lift him out of his bleak and uninspiring existence to an other-worldly consciousness. Like an angel, she plays the "harp" of his body with her "words and gestures" (another religious metaphor).

Like all boys in his position, the narrator desires to speak to his beloved. He contemplates this by entering the room where the priest died and praying—not to God, as might be expected— but to (earthly) love itself: "I pressed the palms of my hands together until they trembled, murmuring: O love! O love! many times."

His prayers are answered in the very next line: "At last she spoke to me." When they speak, they discuss the Oriental fair, Araby, which the girl cannot attend because her school's religious retreat prevents her.

When the narrator promises to bring Mangan's sister a present, he is instantly overwhelmed by the importance of this task, since he hopes a gift will validate his love for her. The quest for the gift is also important symbolically. Araby is a festival with a vaguely Oriental-Middle Eastern ambience. As any Christian at Joyce's time would know, believers in the Middle Ages sometimes made pilgrimages to the holy land, usually bringing back a token or relic as a symbol of religious devotion. Joyce creates a parallel here between the narrator and the early Christian pilgrims—both seeking to bring back a relic to symbolize their devotion, the latter a love for Christ, the former a love for the girl. This replacement of the girl for God clarifies for the reader that the boy has abandoned Christianity in hopes of substituting it with earthly love.

As the day of the fete draws nearer and the commitment becomes more real, however, the reader notices a foreshadowing of negative events. The boy, worried that his uncle will forget, cannot wait to see the sister at the parlour window. Though this might seem trivial, he interprets it pessimistically: "The air was pitilessly raw and already my heart misgave me."

By evening, when the uncle tarries before coming home, the aunt suggests he forget about the fair, "for this night of Our Lord." Although it is Saturday, the evening of the Sabbath, the boy will certainly not substitute religious piety for this extremely important journey to Araby. His boring religious schooling, an uncle who returns home late (and drunk), and his aunt's irritating and pious visitor all highlight the lack of importance religion plays in this boy's life.

The train to Araby is deserted, and the gloomy ride foreshadows the negative aspect of the boy's mission. Once there, the narrator sees that the fair is dark and empty, with an atmosphere "like that of a church after a service." Like the dead priest, the empty church further symbolizes the emptiness of religion in the boy's

life. The analogy to an empty church after mass is underscored by the counting of coins, which also takes place after a mass, except that this hall represents an ordinary commercial event, not the site of spiritual fulfillment. Therefore, the narrator has "difficulty remembering why [he] had come."

After examining the insignificant little gifts at the counter, the boy notices the English accents of two men and a woman flirting and speaking shallowly about the woman's "fib." This word, a euphemism for "lying," emphasizes the lie the boy suddenly understands he is living. He experiences an epiphany when he realizes that no gift will allow him to substitute the love of a common girl for the lost love of a God in which he no longer believes. Although he lingers, "to make [his] interest in her wares seem more real," he recognizes that his pilgrimage to Araby for love and fulfillment is "useless," that he has—in fact—been deceiving himself.

When he hears a voice calling that the "light was out," the boy is indeed in the dark about the meaning of spirituality, having failed to find it both in heaven and on earth. This recognition of his own vain and pretentious notions allows him to see himself as he really is: deluded, with little hope of saving himself. Though the epiphany is a painful and lasting one (remember that the narrator still recalls it as an adult), the boy *has* learned something about his own nature and the danger of attempting to fool oneself with false hopes. His "anguish and anger" are directed toward himself.

Study Questions

1. Knowing how important religious symbols are in "Araby," what do you make of the "wild garden" in the boy's backyard, with its "central apple-tree"?

2. The first sentence of "Araby" describes the Christian Brothers' School "set[ting] the boys free" at the day's end. How is this wording significant?

3. Although the narrator is madly in love with Mangan's sister, he reveals this to no one. What does this imply?

4. The narrator says that her name "sprang to his lips [...] in strange prayers and praises which I myself did not understand." Why isn't he able to understand or interpret them?

5. What is the significance of the fact that Mangan's sister cannot attend Araby because of a retreat?

6. After making his promise, the boy loses all interest in learning, stating that he began to "chafe against the work of school." Why does he have this reaction?

7. When the uncle returns home late and is talking to himself, the boy states: "I could interpret these signs." Can you?

8. Although the boy rides in a "special train for the bazaar," its atmosphere doesn't seem very special at all. What is the significance of this?

9. How does the salesgirl treat the narrator?

10. Why doesn't the boy buy anything at the bazaar?

Answers

1. The "wild garden" reminds us of Adam and Eve's sin in the Garden of Eden and the fact that the boy lives in a falsely pious environment. The apple tree, of course, is another symbol of the Garden of Eden.

2. The school releases them at the day's end, but the word "free" reminds us how oppressive Joyce felt a religious education could be.

3. He tells no one because in his emotions he is extremely isolated from everyone.

4. The boy has not understood for himself his attempt to substitute the young girl's love for the love of God. Therefore, he doesn't understand why her name is mingled with prayers.

5. Formal religion interferes with the narrator's pursuit of her, isolating him further. Again, it recalls the oppressiveness Joyce saw in the Catholic church.

6. He reacts this way because he considers school "child's play" and the love he feels for Mangan's sister is an intense adult love.

7. The uncle is drunk.

8. The train's empty and tawdry atmosphere shows us how isolated the boy is in his quest, and also how unlikely it is that he'll find spiritual fulfillment at the fair.

9. She treats him with disdain and looks over her shoulder at him because she suspects he might steal something. This symbolizes the British and Irish dislike and distrust for each other.

10. He buys nothing because he realizes suddenly how futile his quest is, how impossible it would be to find cosmic fulfillment in the love of an ordinary teenage girl.

Suggested Essay Topics

1. The narrator is bitterly disappointed at the end of the story. Do you believe he has "set himself up" for this disappointment, or did external events cause this to happen? Explain.

2. Bearing in mind the narrator's disappointment at the story's end, might anything positive arise from this painful revelation? Elaborate on what you feel might be the consequences.

Eveline

New Characters:

Eveline Hill: *young woman, 18–20 years old*

Eveline's Father: *an alcoholic*

Eveline's Mother: *who died and Eveline loved*

Frank: *Eveline's betrothed*

Summary

Nearly all the events in this story take place in Eveline Hill's mind as she prepares to run away from her father's home and elope with a sailor. About 18–20 years old, Eveline has supported and cared for her alcoholic father for an unspecified number of years after her mother's death. Although her existence is described in her thoughts as extremely empty, she has profound misgivings about leaving: her duty to her father, her promise to her dying mother that she would look after the home, and the fear of making such a significant change in her life all appear to immobilize her.

Finally, when Eveline reaches the port where her fiance is waiting and where their ship will depart, she's overcome by inertia and can't leave with him, although he begs her.

Analysis

The protagonist and namesake of this story is not named by the author until the last few lines of the story. This should indicate to the reader that Eveline Hill does not possess a fully-developed sense of self; she exists for other people, and this is the crux of her dilemma.

Eveline sits at the window, tired, inert, and considering the "rather happy" times of her youth, although she is still only a young woman. Many of the most important or uplifting people in her life are dead: her brother, her friends, and most significantly her mother, whose spirit and memory keep Eveline where she is. Having promised her mother that she would "keep the home together as long as she could," Eveline is torn between enduring the misery of her father's alcoholism and escaping to a life with her betrothed. Regardless of the fact that she has tried as hard as she could, Eveline still feels indebted to her mother's memory and cannot move herself out of the paralysis that keeps her tied to this pathetic existence.

Looking around the room at familiar objects, she cannot conceive "where on earth all the dust came from." This allusion is Biblical, reminding us that we begin from and return to dust after our deaths. The image of death—spiritual and physical—pervades Eveline's consciousness as the dust pervades her household.

The parlour of their house is dreary, decorated by a few meaningless objects and the print of Blessed Margaret Mary Alacoque. This seventeenth-century saint epitomized suffering for the love of Christ, inflicting wounds upon herself and taking it upon herself to endure great trials, for she believed that the holy father wished her to assume the burden of others' misery. That Eveline looks and prays to Saint Margaret Mary indicates the degree of suffering which she feels she must endure in order to be a good

Christian and dutiful daughter. Joyce obviously does not condone her feelings, since Eveline suffers abuse from her father and degradation at work—both with little rewards.

The parallels and contrasts between Eveline's father and her intended warn the reader that no route Eveline takes is a guarantee to happiness. She considers her father, though abusive, to be nice "sometimes," having to reach far back in her memory to an event at which he behaved even remotely lovingly. While Frank obviously feels more tender about her, Eveline's feelings are not as clear: when he sings to her, she feels "pleasantly confused," and this feeling she confuses with affection. Indeed, love between them never crosses her mind, for the relationship evolved first as "an excitement for her to have a fellow and then she had begun to like him." Her inability to respond to Frank's kindness indicates that her sacrifices have robbed her of life-giving emotions, and that—without change—her existence will be devoid of any meaning whatsoever.

The only love Eveline can clearly recognize is that for her dead mother, but this is suffused with guilt, which Eveline assuages by sacrificing her own happiness. Although the mother is no longer alive, she ironically exhibits the greatest force in the story; her daughter is so passive that she seems on the point of (spiritual) death. Indeed, as the time draws near for her to meet Frank, she recognizes that "[h]er time was running out." Significantly, Eveline can identify the futility of her mother's life as "commonplace sacrifices closing in final craziness," but is unable to see the sacrifices that this life is currently causing for her.

When Eveline goes to the quay with Frank, the ship's portholes are illuminated as if to cast a bright light on her escape route. Nevertheless, Eveline feels numb, in "a maze of distress" over her departure from this life, and prays to God for direction. Understanding that she worships Saint Margaret Mary, the reader knows that Eveline believes all sacrifice is holy; her mother martyred herself for the family as the saint sacrificed herself for her religion. Therefore, Eveline determines that her own salvation and happiness mean nothing in light of her mother's dreadful pull upon her and her obligation toward suffering. Significantly and for the first time, Frank calls out Eveline's name in the story, since he is the only one in her life to value her for herself, but she cannot respond. Terrified at the prospect of actually deciding her own destiny, Eveline stands "passive, like a helpless animal" and does not return his affection or even his appeals. Importantly, when Frank is drawn into the crowd, Eveline looks at him with neither affection, farewell, nor even recognition, since she is—in effect—spiritually dead and completely unable to generate emotion.

Study Questions

1. What is the overwhelming characteristic of Eveline's youthful memories?

2. Explain the significance of the nameless priest whose photo hangs on the wall.

3. Frank's background is given, but he's not physically described. Why not?

4. How can we tell that Eveline is not in love?

5. What is the significance of all the "dust" in the house?

6. Why is Eveline's job at the Stores mentioned?

7. Why does Eveline find her life not "undesirable" at the moment she's about to leave it?

8. Explain the significance of the Italian organ player's music when Eveline is getting ready to leave.

9. Eveline is afraid both to go with Frank and to turn him away, especially "after all he had done for her." What does this imply?

10. At the end of the story, Eveline clings to the gate and won't follow Frank. Interpret this.

Answers

1. Everyone Eveline truly cared about is dead.

2. The father cares so little about his religion that he doesn't even bother to remember the priest's name. It is an empty symbol to him.

3. Eveline is so numb to the concept of love that Frank is hardly a reality to her. He's a means of escape, but not one of which she avails herself.

4. Eveline believes "she had begun to like" Frank, but this is the only emotion mentioned regarding him. She also doesn't think of him in physical terms.

5. According to the Bible, we are made from dust and to dust we return. The dust in the home represents death.

6. In her position at the Stores, she's treated like a servant, just as she is at home. There is no outlet for her, and no place where she feels her own significance.

7. She so fears change that her subconsciousness is attempting to convince her that her life isn't that bad. In reality, of course, it's unbearable.

8. The foreign music indicates a foreign influence and Eveline's potential escape from her life and Dublin with Frank.

9. Eveline bases her responses on obligations to other people: her father, her (dead) mother, her (dead) brother, etc. Frank has come to symbolize just another obligation, but not romantic love.

10. She is literally and figuratively paralyzed; fear of change has frozen her in her current life.

Suggested Essay Topics

1. Discuss the parallels and differences between Frank's role in Eveline's life and her father's role.

2. Joyce juxtaposes an image of the mother's final delirium and Eveline's concept of "escape." Discuss why these two images are next to one another in the story.

After the Race

New Characters:

Jimmy Doyle: *wealthy 20–21 year-old Irishman*

Charles Segouin: *owner of a French race car, his friend*

Andre Riviere: *friend of Segouin*

Villona: *Hungarian friend of Segouin*

Routh: *English friend of Segouin*

Farley: *American friend of Riviere*

Summary

The story begins with a young, wealthy Dublin college graduate, Jimmy Doyle, engaging in a motor car race through Dublin with three Europeans from the continent: two Frenchmen and a Hungarian. Although Jimmy's family is known in Dublin for its wealth, among the sophisticated Europeans, he is more in awe of them than their equal, and he is thrilled at being seen in their company by his Irish friends.

After the race, Jimmy attends a dinner at the home of Segouin, the owner of the race car, where he meets an English friend of Segouin and talks about Irish politics. But before the conversation can become serious, the host interrupts and the group goes for a walk in the streets. Meeting an American friend of Riviere, the men drink, carouse and return to Segouin's to play cards. Playing far into the night, Jimmy loses a considerable, but unspecified, amount of money due to his drinking and lack of gambling skill. Nevertheless, he continues to be dazzled by the international suavity of the group until daybreak comes and the debts are calculated.

Analysis

Of all the stories in his collection, Joyce felt that "After the Race" was among the least successful. The story of Jimmy Doyle and his careless wealth is a bit cliched; his international playboy friends are also somewhat predictable. At the heart of the story, though, is Dublin within an international arena, aching to be recognized on its own, even if the price of that recognition is exploitation. Jimmy's story is Dublin's (and Ireland's) in microcosm, although Jimmy is substantially wealthier than the other Dubliners in this collection. When the reader learns more about him, we discover that Jimmy's father was "an advanced [Irish] nationalist" but moderated his views early, only then gaining his wealth. Significantly, that wealth allowed Jimmy an upbringing far removed from native Irish traditions: he attended school in England, studied at Dublin University (the prestigious Protestant college in Dublin with close British ties), and then returned to Cambridge (England) to "see a little life." Thus, the life to which Jimmy is exposed is hardly an Irish one, despite his father's early nationalist leanings.

Consequently, Jimmy's acquaintances (whom he considers friends) in the race car are an international group, for he finds great pleasure in those who have "seen so much of the world." Indeed, everything about the race through Dublin, described as a "channel of poverty and inaction" along the racing route, exhilarates Jimmy. Not once does he realize that the cheering crowds of the "gratefully oppressed" represent his kinship with the city; he much more willingly identifies with Segouin and his *bon vivant* crowd. Having been seen in this company, Jimmy enjoys his condescending return to the "profane world of spectators" and basks in their admiration of his status, wealth, and worldliness.

Yet amid the worldliness, Jimmy is still a Dubliner hoping for recognition from the outside world. He and his parents feel "pride" and "eagerness" as Jimmy anticipates the sophisticated dinner at Segouin's home. Once there, he's dazzled by the company and conversation, although the description of the latter is hardly harmonious. When the British Routh's comments awaken the "buried" nationalist zeal of Jimmy's father in the younger Doyle, the reader imagines that Jimmy might identify with the Irish at last. Rather, Segouin proposes an ironic toast to "Humanity" and Jimmy's momentary flash of nationalism disappears.

As the night continues and more friends are encountered, Jimmy finds himself awash in an international sea of cosmopolitan debauchery. To his naive mind, the silly dancing and drinking songs are tantamount to "seeing life," yet the author adds the additional thought "at least." With this, Joyce indicates Jimmy's vague

doubts about the value of the "merriment," but he suppresses these doubts as he did his earlier feelings of nationalism.

Feelings of doubt also infiltrate Jimmy's thoughts regarding his business venture in Segouin's motor car, a deal which translated into "days' work that lordly car in which he sat" earlier in the afternoon. He and his father both support the deal, but the author shrewdly keeps the extent of Jimmy's financial involvement ambiguous; the reader is made to feel uneasy about the investment's security. If Jimmy's ego were not so easily flattered by Segouin's attentions, Joyce intimates, Jimmy might feel more alert—and more uneasy as well.

The insecurity of the investment is re-figured at the end of the story in the group's night of card playing. Reckless and unskilled, Jimmy knows he's outmatched by the experienced Europeans but is "glad of the dark stupor that would cover up his folly." Apparently, the privilege of being swindled by sophisticated continentals more than makes up for his crushing losses. Significantly, Routh—the British guest—wins the game, symbolizing Britain's exploitation of Ireland in international affairs. The "Daybreak!" call at the story's end indicates that Jimmy must now face the unpleasant consequences of having been defrauded by his "friends," just as Ireland, Joyce suggests, must awaken to the realities of its own exploitation by foreign powers.

Study Questions

1. Interpret the significance of Jimmy's inconsistent education.

2. Why is it meaningful that Jimmy's father becomes wealthy only after he abandons his patriotic beliefs?

3. Jimmy's investment in Segouin's racecar is ambiguously described. Why has the author failed to provide further details?

4. Interpret the sentence: "Rapid motion through space elates one; so does notoriety; so does the possession of money."

5. What's ironic about Seguouin's toast to "Humanity"?

6. The story describes the circuitous route taken by the "friends" as they wander around after the race. What is the symbolism implied in their wandering?

7. While they celebrate, the author writes that Dublin harbor "lay like a darkened mirror at their feet." Is there significance in this?

8. Why does Jimmy's father, a shrewd businessman, not question Jimmy's investment more carefully?

9. Why is Jimmy unconcerned about his heavy losses at cards?

10. Why is it Villona who shouts, "Daybreak, gentlemen!"

Answers

1. The inconsistency signifies that Jimmy lacks focus; the overwhelmingly British influence of his education shows us that Jimmy's family doesn't value Irish culture.

2. This symbolizes the impoverished Irish nationalist movement.

3. The investment is obviously risky; it's likely that its details are also ambiguous to Jimmy himself.

4. With his "rapid motion," Jimmy is staving off paralysis; his fame and wealth also help him escape the fate of the other Dubliners in this book.

5. He interrupts with the toast so that Routh and Jimmy will not argue about Irish independence.

6. The group—like Jimmy himself—lacks direction.

7. One cannot see anything in a "darkened mirror." Jimmy can't discern the true nature of these "friends," who are about to swindle him in cards.

8. He's so eager for his son to be a social success that he's willing to risk a poor investment.

9. Like his father, Jimmy is so eager to enter into a cosmopolitan European world that he's willing to let himself be exploited.

10. Villona, who has no money, doesn't gamble. He's the only one to see the light of day, but now it's time for Jimmy to recognize the reality of things as well.

1. Explain the parallel relationship(s) between Jimmy's heavy gambling losses, his ambiguous investment, and his father's support of that investment.

2. Interpret the line during the young men's "merriment" when the author tells us: "Jimmy took his part with a will; this was seeing life, at least!"

Two Gallants

New Characters:

Corley: *a womanizer about 25 years old*

Lenehan: *his buddy, approximately the same age*

Servant Girl ("Slavey"): *whom Corley is dating*

Summary

The story commences as Corley and Lenehan are walking through Dublin at the end of the workday, discussing Corley's exploits with women and passing time before Corley's date. Currently, he is involved with a servant girl (a "slavey") whom he uses and has sex with but has no intention of marrying. Lenehan enjoys listening but offers little judgment and no stories of his own.

As they pass a club, they hear a harpist on the street playing an Irish folksong to a crowd. Soon thereafter, Corley spots the servant girl, whom Lenehan looks over in appraisal. After the two leave on their date, Lenehan walks aimlessly through the city, eats dinner at a cheap shop, and continues to think about Corley's exploits and audaciousness with the girl.

Finally, after the time at which they'd agreed to meet, Lenehan spots Corley as he walks the girl home. He sees her enter the house, come out cautiously for a moment, and then return. Lenehan is so overwhelmed with curiosity that he calls out to the now-solitary Corley, who at first doesn't answer him. Ultimately, Corley smiles and shows Lenehan the gold coin in his hand, which the servant has given to him.

Analysis

The late addition of this story to *Dubliners* caused delays in the book's publication, for Corley's casual attitude toward sex and the men's use of profanity (which Joyce agreed to omit) disquieted both the book's printer and publisher. Joyce remained adamant, however, and the story was included.

The ironic nature of this story is immediately obvious in the title; Corley and Lenehan are not "gallants" but coarse, manipulative figures. Both men are grotesque. Corley is obnoxious and self-centered, staring "as if he were on parade," concerned only with his ego and physical gratification. Lenehan is a talker but not a doer; his "tongue was tired for he had been talking all afternoon," but he has no similar stories of womanizing to share with Corley. Rather, he looks up to Corley with wonder throughout the story and in the end is described as Corley's "disciple." Whereas Corley is brutish and aggressive in an exaggeratedly macho sense, Lenehan suggests the same extreme in opposite form. His "air of gentility" and ineffectual bearing suggest his emasculated character. His need to follow Corley like a puppy shows us his lack of initiative or ability for independent thought.

Corley delights in the attention of his follower, drawing out for Lenehan tales of his exploits with women, all of which highlight Corley's lack of humanism (not to mention manners!) and kindness. When he discusses his current prospect, a servant girl whom he terms a "slavey," he boasts of all he has gotten from her: cigarettes, cigars, and sex. He fears temporarily that she'll become pregnant, but protects himself by concealing his true identity, which also protects his power in their relationship.

When he later discusses a former girlfriend who is presently "on the turf" (a prostitute), Lenehan suggests that Corley is responsible for the woman's downfall. Corley—predictably—abdicates responsibility. The juxtaposed images of the prostitute and the current "slavey," as well as Lenehan's description of his friend as a "base betrayer," indicate to the reader the servant girl's probable fate should she remain loyal to Corley. His power over her is further evidenced by the fact that he always "lets her wait a bit" for their rendezvous.

While still anticipating meeting the slavey, the two men stop before the club on Kildare Street (known in Joyce's time as an exclusive Anglo-Irish club) to listen to a harpist playing "Silent, O Moyle." The harp traditionally symbolizes Ireland and the ballad is a folksong about Fionnuala, the Irish daughter of the sea. It is an ironic paradox that these two powerful Irish symbols are employed to solicit spare change on a street corner in front of an Anglo-Irish club. Significant too is the author's description and personification of the harp itself: "[h]eedless that her coverings had fallen about her knees" and "weary of the eyes of stranger." The harp, like the servant girl friend of Corley, are both being prostituted for insignificant reward; both are "weary" and accustomed to careless treatment. As A. Walton Litz points out, the slavey and the harp "represent Ireland's contemporary subjugation," the former by Corley, the latter by England (375).

This point is furthered when Lenehan later looks over the slavey just as the passersby glance heedlessly at the harpist on the corner. The girl, dressed in "Sunday finery" of blue and white, wears the traditional colors of the Virgin Mary, but the "contented leer" of her smile and Corley's graphic assessment of her guarantee to the reader that she does not represent Catholic Ireland's purity.

After Corley departs, Lenehan's energy leaves him; his face looks older and his spirits darken. More thoughtful than Corley, Lenehan senses that the aimless wandering through Dublin streets and meaningless exchanges with women won't fulfill him. His vision of Corley seducing the slavey makes Lenehan "feel keenly his own poverty of purse and spirit," but he does not understand that following Corley is an unsuitable—ultimately unsatisfying—preoccupation for him.

Lenehan is obsessed over Corley's success with the girl, so much so that the reader believes Lenehan to be gaining vicarious pleasure (perhaps even erotic pleasure) from his imaginings. Repeatedly, he wonders "had Corley managed it successfully," experiencing "all the pangs and thrills of his friend's situation." The reader undoubtedly believes that Corley is attempting to have sex with the slavey, yet his earlier concern with her potential pregnancy leads us to believe that they have already consummated the affair.

Lenehan is so excited to see Corley at the evening's end that he can hardly contain himself—so anxious is he to know the

outcome. The reader, too, wants to know the extent of Corley's success. Like the arrogant brute he is, though, Corley keeps Lenehan and the reader waiting for his answer, and at the very last minute pompously shows his "disciple" (and us) the gold coin that the slavey has stolen for him.

That the girl debases herself both in stealing and in paying for Corley's affection brings the theme back to Ireland's degradation, for the slavey represents the Irish peasant who is exploited in her attempt to eke out a satisfactory life for herself. Corley profits from her weakness and needs; Lenehan—weaker and less cunning than Corley—looks on admiringly.

Study Questions

1. What is the symbolism of the "veiled moon" in this story?

2. Is there religious significance in Lenehan's repeated statement that Corley's exploits "take the biscuit"?

3. What effect can we draw from Corley's always walking "as if he were on parade"?

4. Corley used to date a higher class of girls before he started dating a "slavey." Why has he "traded down"?

5. The slavey is wearing blue and white for their date, the traditional colors of the Virgin Mary. What is the meaning of this?

6. After Corley leaves him, Lenehan is famished. What's the significance of this?

7. Rather than just having encounters, Lenehan would like to "settle down" and "live happily." What's the importance of this?

8. Joyce goes to great lengths to represent Lenehan's wandering route through the Dublin streets. Why?

9. Beyond the fact that the slavey's stealing money for him is immoral, how does it connect to the fact that Corley's former girlfriend is now "on the turf"?

10. Lenehan imagines "Corley's voice in deep energetic gallantries." What's the irony in this?

Answers

1. The moon is traditionally a romantic image, but Corley's treatment is abusive and contemptible; it's hardly romantic.

2. Lenehan is Corley's disciple in the underhanded treatment of women. Therefore, the "biscuit" referred to represents the Holy Eucharist.

3. He is very conceited and self-absorbed.

4. Women with less money and no education are easier for Corley to manipulate and less demanding.

5. The symbolism is ironic; the slavey is not pure and probably not a virgin if she's involved with Corley.

6. Corley's exploits are titillating but not emotionally satisfying for Lenehan because they are empty. He longs for something more meaningful.

7. Although he admires Corley in a perverse way, Lenehan is a very different person, as is evidenced by Lenehan's mild criticism of Corley's "adventures."

8. Torn between Corley's way of life and his own desires, Lenehan leads a directionless and "wandering" existence."

9. Both women have been lead to commit crimes through Corley's negative influence.

10. Corley is no gallant; Lenehan only imagines that he has that potential.

Suggested Essay Topics

1. Joyce's description of Corley is overly male or macho, while Lenehan seems more effeminate. What is the meaning of this polarity among the two friends?

2. What attitude does Lenehan demonstrate throughout the story regarding Corley's abuses of women? Does he approve, disapprove, or is he torn? Explain his emotional stance.

The Boarding House

New Characters:

Mrs. Mooney: *owner of the boarding house*

Polly Mooney: *her 19-year-old daughter*

Bob Doran: *boarder with whom Polly has become romantically involved*

Summary

Polly Mooney, 19, lives in her mother's boarding house with her brother and the young male boarders and tourists who make up its inhabitants. Polly is pretty, and she receives flirtatious advances from many of the boarders and reciprocates, but Mrs. Mooney is frustrated by her daughter's lack of progress in finding a husband. When Polly begins to have a not-too-subtle affair with one of the boarders, Bob Doran, Mrs. Mooney stays surprisingly quiet and her daughter wonders if she's acquiescent. In fact, Mrs. Mooney waits until the relationship between them is quite advanced before she decides to talk—first to Polly and then to the young man.

When Polly turns to Bob, she confesses that she's frightened of her mother's suspicions and the consequences of their situation; Bob reassures her limply. Soon thereafter, Mrs. Mooney asks to speak with Bob in private. Although he understands the content of their meeting and feels full of dread, he complies.

Meanwhile, Polly composes herself in her room and relaxes as she thinks of her liaisons with Bob. When her mother calls her from below, she tells Polly to come downstairs because Bob wants to speak with her. The reader never learns the exact content of either of the two conversations.

Analysis

The overt theme of prostitution in "The Two Gallants" is played out more subtly in Mrs. Mooney's boarding house. Joyce begins the story with a synopsis of Mrs. Mooney's dreadful marriage: struggling to succeed as a woman in a patriarchal society, she married

Mr. Mooney and suffered through his alcoholism and ruinous business practices. Owing to Mrs. Mooney's common sense and ferocious determination, she succeeds in spite of her husband, running a boarding house and supporting her family. Thus, it's highly ironic that Mrs. Mooney—having been almost destroyed in a wretched marriage—is so eager to enter her daughter, Polly, into a union that is flawed at best and disastrous at worst.

Having looked over the many boarders with whom Polly has flirted, her mother decides that Bob Doran is the most likely marital prospect among them. Therefore, even when Polly and Bob's liaison becomes obvious in the house, Mrs. Mooney pretends not to notice. If she noticed, her obligation as a Christian and mother would force her to demand its end. If she doesn't recognize the affair, she can let it progress so far that Doran will have no option but to marry Polly when confronted. In effect, Mrs. Mooney allows Polly to sell herself to Doran in exchange for the marital obligation he will ultimately owe her. The arrangement is a manipulative and exploitive one, highlighting Mrs. Mooney's nickname among the boarders as "The Madam," since she's prostituting her daughter.

As far as Polly's culpability in the arrangement is concerned, she senses her mother's plan and cooperates tacitly with it. The song she sings ("I'm a naughty girl.../You know I am") indicates her character, and her brazen seduction of the meek Bob Doran shows the reader that Polly has inherited her mother's determination. With Bob, however, Polly behaves timidly and remorsefully; she leans on him to assume the burden of guilt and fear, and Bob ambivalently complies. The reader should rightfully suspect Polly's meekness, since she has already identified herself as a "naughty girl," and the author describes her as resembling "a little perverse madonna." This contrasts ludicrously with the hapless and limp image she presents to Doran; the reader can easily see the disingenuousness of this guise. Further, the description of Polly at the story's end shows a fully composed woman reliving the "secret amiable memories" of her tryst with Doran. Far from penitent, Polly is portrayed as a sensual woman relaxing at the very scene of her seduction.

Polly's melodramatic reaction over the situation only heightens Doran's guilt and recognition that "reparation must be made for such a sin." The term reparation means financial repayment, but it also bears a religious meaning: the amendment(s) made to God for sinful acts. Doran thinks of this affair as a sin, and his career with a Catholic employer demands that he maintain a spotless record. He has discussed penance with a priest in terms of seeking "a loophole of reparation" but realizes that under the circumstances, the church allows him no option besides marriage.

It is significant that Doran wants to amend the sin only to secure his position and not for the sake of his soul. Likewise, Mrs. Mooney and her daughter see amendment for the "sin" in financial terms, since Bob has a "good screw" (job) and "a bit of stuff" (savings) as well. Considering the situation, Mrs. Mooney's thoughts are appropriate for a deal-maker or gambler rather than a mother concerned with her child's honor: "[s]he felt sure she would win" and deals with moral problems "as a cleaver deals with meat."

Doran's situation is hopeless, since Mrs. Mooney knows she has Catholic tradition and Irish societal values on her side. In this, Joyce condemns the parochial Irish beliefs that would force a marriage between so unlikely a pair. Polly, for her part, leaves the direct confrontation to her capable mother and manipulates Bob in more beguiling and subtle ways. Because of this tradition and its flaws, the author tells us, both Polly and Bob are doomed to unhappiness, as was Polly's mother when she married out of financial necessity years before.

Study Questions

1. What is implied in the fact that Polly couldn't continue to work in the corn-factor's office?

2. Why is Mrs. Mooney so intent on her daughter marrying practically anyone?

3. How innocent was Polly's initial approach to Bob Doran?

4. Interpret the statement: "She was an outraged mother."

5. The "short twelve" Mrs. Mooney hopes to catch after her conversation is the abbreviated noon-time mass. What's the symbolism implied in this?

6. Bob seeks religious counsel after the affair has become serious. What is the irony in this?

7. Why is Polly's brother physically described before Bob talks to Mrs. Mooney?

8. Why does Joyce continually refer to Bob's glasses becoming dim with moisture?

9. Why is the maid's name Mary?

10. Why does Polly forget "what she had been waiting for"?

Answers

1. Due to her loose morals, she probably began a liaison with the "disreputable sheriff's man."

2. Without a husband, a young woman had absolutely no value and no rights at this time in society. In Mrs. Mooney's eyes, a poor match was better than no husband at all.

3. Not very innocent at all. The clothing she wore (combined with her history as a flirt) leads us to believe it was calculated.

4. If Mrs. Mooney were outraged, she would have acted sooner and prevented the affair. She is merely using her mock outrage as leverage against Bob.

5. The spiritual content of the mass means nothing to her, which is why she hopes to catch the shortened version of it. There's further irony in her hoping to attend mass after she's prostituted her daughter.

6. Bob doesn't care about the state of his soul so much as he does about his status at work.

7. Jack is physically threatening and Bob fears him; this is another reason why he'll acquiesce to Mrs. Mooney's demand.

8. Bob so fears the consequences of his discussion with Mrs. Mooney that he is close to tears.

9. In this house of mock prostitution, it's ironic that the maid shares the same name as the Blessed Virgin.

10. Like Bob, Polly has no free will; she isn't waiting for anything because the decision is completely in her mother's hands.

Suggested Essay Topics

1. Discuss the ironic parallels between Mrs. Mooney's marital situation (as a young woman) and her daughter's current situation.

2. Waiting for Mrs. Mooney's demand, Bob thinks to himself: "Perhaps they could be happy together...." Considering the situation, prognosticate the likelihood of a successful marriage between Polly and Bob Doran.

A Little Cloud

New Characters:

Little Chandler: *Thirty-ish clerk and amateur poet*

Ignatius Gallaher: *Little Chandler's school friend, now a journalist living in London*

Little's Wife (Annie) and Baby Son

Summary

Little Chandler, a 30-year-old legal clerk, is anticipating his evening meeting with Ignatius Gallaher, a friend from his youth. In the eight years since they've seen each other, Gallaher has moved to London to become a journalist, a situation which both impresses Little and makes him envious. He covets Gallaher's freedom to travel as well as his career as a writer. As he prepares for their meeting, Little allows himself to hope that Gallaher might be able to help him launch a literary career as a poet, perhaps even outside of Dublin.

Gallaher, however, talks mostly about himself—not about Little's literary ambitions—and Chandler finds his manner slightly vulgar, especially when discussing the immorality that abounds abroad. After several more drinks than Little's customary number, they discuss Little's wife and baby son. Although Gallaher congratulates him he swears that he would never marry and, at the end of their last drink, patronizes the entire notion of marriage.

When Chandler returns home he argues with his wife about a petty complaint and she leaves him with the baby to run an errand. Alone with his son, Chandler begins to resent and regret the different elements of his life that he believes are holding him back. As Little reads poetry and considers the likelihood of a career as a writer, his child wakes up screaming and cannot be comforted. His wife returns, furious that Little has disturbed the child. As she comforts the baby, Little's own eyes begin to fill with tears.

Analysis

Joyce drew the title for this story from I Kings 18:44. The prophet Elijah, having defeated false prophets and returned his people to the Lord, announces that the end of a long drought is at hand: "there ariseth a little cloud out of the sea, like a man's hand." The long drought of Little Chandler's life and career, however, shows no sign of ending in the story.

Throughout the story, Thomas Chandler is described in infantile terms, highlighting for the reader his ineffectual presence. He is "fragile," his voice "quiet," and he has "childish white teeth." His nickname, of course, articulates his overly-boyish qualities, as do the author's descriptions of his "infant hope" and adolescent shyness both with Gallaher and his wife.

Little dreams of being a poet, but even his dreams are unassuming: "If he could give expression to it in a book of poems perhaps men would listen," he thinks, and longs to establish a "little circle of kindred minds." (emphasis added) It's clear to the reader that Little has dim hopes of taking the literary world by storm; the author tells us that "he was not sure what idea he wished to express" with his writing, and his career as a poet (and the poems themselves) are sketchily conceived. His reading of Byron at the story's end and his longing to "write like that" are absurd given his nature; Byron's romantic and daring persona represent the complete antithesis of Little's juvenile character and bearing.

When we meet at last the highly-anticipated Ignatius Gallaher, we can see immediately that he offers no hope in amending Little's

dilemma. Crude, unhealthy-looking, and boorish, Gallaher seems to have returned to "dear dirty Dublin" merely to patronize the city and brag to his awestruck friends. Gallaher is portrayed as a non-believer and drunkard. When Little questions him timidly about the immoral nature of Paris, Gallaher makes a "catholic gesture with his right arm," as if blessing the tawdriness found on the continent. Gallaher also encourages Little to "liquor up" beyond his ability, and Little—in an attempt to impress Gallaher with his man-liness—drinks beyond his measure. For his part, Gallaher is described by Joyce as "emerging from clouds of smoke." His discussion of his journalist's life in Europe is full of allusions to alcohol: "it's a rum world," he tells Little. "Talk of immorality! I've heard of cases—what am I saying?—I've known them: cases of…immorality." (emphasis added)

While at first Little is overwhelmed by Gallaher's experience, he finds himself justifiably "disillusioned" with his friend and finds in his manner "something vulgar […] which he had not observed before." He also finally sees—long after the reader has noticed it—that Gallaher is "patronizing [Little] by his friendliness just as he was patronizing Ireland by his visit." Gallaher obviously visits Dublin to crow among his friends and feel superior, but Gallaher's unbridled bitterness towards life and his drinking indicate his own dissatisfaction with himself. Although Gallaher boasts of financial opportunities with women and attempts to glamorize the sinful-ness of the continent, the reader—and even Little himself—sees through this pretense.

When Gallaher denigrates the idea of marriage, Little initially defends the practice, but later has no response, as he begins to agree with Gallaher's crude that it "must get a bit stale" over time. Having had too many drinks, Little worries that he has "betrayed himself" regarding his own unhappiness, yet threatens Gallaher by telling him: "You'll put your head in the sack…like everyone else."

Returning home to his wife, Annie, Little cannot stop re-play-ing his meeting with his former friend and the bitterness it inspired within him. Considering the differences between their tempera-ments, Little questions why Gallaher has received the lucky breaks and not he. "What is it that stood in his way?" he asks himself, answering immediately and correctly: "His unfortunate timidity!" Diagnosing that the problem lies within himself, Little grows even more frustrated with his life, since he recognizes that he has trapped himself with his "pretty" wife and furniture—neither of which continue to satisfy. When he considers escaping to London, he immediately becomes bogged down by obligations and worries about bill payments for the furniture, demonstrating his inability to imagine himself in a more fulfilling life. As he attempts unsuccessfully to read and calm the child simultaneously, Little's thoughts sum up his futility: "He couldn't read. He couldn't do anything....He was a prisoner for life."

Little's baby boy is an ironic comment on his own lack of maturity. Since Little has been described throughout the story as infantile, it seems almost impossible that he can adequately fulfill a father's role. Indeed, Little has obvious trouble in this capacity, since he cannot comfort his child and fears that his own incompetency may bring about its death.

When Annie rushes in, she shrieks at Little for his paltry skills, and he responds by stammering excuses like a terrified schoolboy. He can control neither the child's sobbing, nor his wife's temper, nor his own life.

Annie soothes her son, calling him a "little man" and speaking babytalk. Ironically, her husband is a little man whose marriage to an emasculating woman has even further diminished his ability and confidence. The author hints that Annie's suffocating love for the boy may turn him into a grown-up child like his father. Finally, at the story's end, we see how Annie's love has quieted the baby, but her resentment of Little—and his overwhelming despair at his situation—brings child-like tears to his own eyes, and the two males in the narrative have ironically reversed situations.

Study Questions

1. Why is Little made to appear so juvenile in the story?

2. What is the significance of Gallaher's working for the London press?

3. Interpret the line about Little: "At times he repeated the lines [of poetry] to himself and this consoled him."

4. Thinking of his meeting with Gallaher, Little feels "superior" to others "for the first time in his life." Why and what does this represent?

5. The restaurant where Gallaher is to meet Little is a swanky spot, where the waiters "spoke French and German." What's the significance of this?

6. Why is Gallaher described as possessing an "unhealthy pallor"?

7. What does Gallaher's heavy drinking symbolize?

8. Why does Little "allow his whiskey to be very much diluted"?

9. Explain the ironic significance of the two men's very different physical descriptions.

10. What is the irony of Little's tears at the story's end?

Answers

1. This description heightens our sense of his helplessness.

2. Britain ruled Ireland by a hostile and colonial mandate. Most Irish hated England's presence, and allusions to Britain are almost always negative and corrupt symbols in Joyce.

3. Little is content to repeat meaningless motions rather than move forward, the idea of which frightens him.

4. Little feels the reflected glory of his friend. He cannot feel superior because of his own accomplishments.

5. Little assumes that things influenced by continental Europe are naturally superior; he is biased against Dublin and Irish influence.

6. Gallaher's attitude toward life is corrupt and unhealthy.

7. It symbolizes the degree of his dissolution and also his personal dissatisfaction, in spite of all his bragging.

8. Literally, he is not a heavy drinker. Symbolically, Chandler feels an aversion to the Irish influence.

9. Although they are close in age, Gallaher is described as much older-looking. This emphasizes his debauched life, whereas

Little's adolescent appearance emphasizes his innocence and naivete.

10. It is an ironic allusion to Little's helplessness and exaggerated innocence.

Suggested Essay Topics

1. How is Little's situation similar to that experienced by the narrator in "Araby"?

2. Explain the significance of Little's relationship to his wife as portrayed at the end of the story. What is the meaning of the episode with her blouse, and what does it say about Little's relationship to her? To women in general?

Counterparts

New Characters:

Farrington: *Forty-ish clerk and alcoholic*

Mr. Alleyne: *Farrington's boss*

Weathers: *an English entertainer whom Farrington meets in a pub*

Several of Farrington's Drinking Companions

Summary

When the story begins, Farrington, an alcoholic administrator in a law office, is enduring the chastisement of his boss, Mr. Alleyne, for his shabby work. Diving into a pub for a drink to calm his anger, Farrington returns to the office even more muddled than before and makes several more errors in his work. When Alleyne rebukes him, this time in front of a client, Farrington responds insultingly, and the boss nearly goes wild with anger.

Later, Farrington retreats to a bar with his friends. When he retells the scene during which he insulted his boss, Farrington grows obviously more proud of his wit, and the small party of men drinks in celebration. Weathers, a British performer, joins their crowd and allows several of the men to buy him a round of drinks without offering to buy one himself. This annoys Farrington, as money is tight and the Londoner orders expensive drinks. Later, when his friends suggest he arm wrestle with Weathers, Farrington is further annoyed when the performer beats him twice.

Furious that he's out of money and liquor and has been humiliated by a stranger, Farrington returns home in a foul mood. After his young son tells him that his mother has left to attend an evening mass, Farrington unleashes all of his anger on the child and beats him violently.

Analysis

The counterparts in this story are many and transcend the borders of the story itself. Farrington, like Little Chandler, is frustrated in his job and embittered in his marriage. Like Little, Farrington is condescended to (by his boss) and feels trapped by his life circumstances. Little's wife demoralizes him, whereas in "Counterparts" Farrington's boss treats him like an ineffectual nonentity. The endings of the two stories present unsettling parallels as well. Both show us fathers whose family life is out of control, and both end with a child (the son) in tears. However, in "Counterparts," Farrington has actively brought about his son's tears by beating him, and this represents an essential difference between Farrington and Little Chandler.

Unlike Little, Farrington is loathsome, not pathetic: an irresponsible alcoholic whose work and family suffer because of his volcanic temper and self-abuse. In his dealings with the egg-headed Mr. Alleyne, Farrington's self-respect is so diminished that his anger wells up at the very sound of Alleyne's voice. Significantly, Alleyne possesses a "Piercing North of Ireland accent" (suggesting he is Protestant and a British sympathizer). This polarity between the Catholic Farrington and his Protestant boss heightens their animosity. It also sets up the most important counterpart relationship in the story: that between (Protestant) Britain and (Catholic) Ireland.

Having scurried out of his office for a furtive drink, Farrington cannot concentrate on his work, makes even more mistakes, and brings Alleyne's growing wrath down upon him once again. When Alleyne insults and yells at him, Farrington—his tongue loosened

by alcohol—responds with an insulting and surprisingly witty re-mark. Farrington feels emboldened by this "victory" over the boss, but cannot grasp that angering Alleyne will only engender more troubles for him. This, too, resembles Ireland's situation with the British: minor, trivial victories against the Empire would not gain meaningful freedom, just more abuse.

Reliving the incident with his friends in a pub makes Farrington feel like a man—not a groveling office boy—for the first time in the narrative, but only temporarily and only when he's drinking. This signifies to us the meager sense of self that Farrington actually possesses. When the British artiste Weathers joins the drinking men, Farrington is obliged to buy a round of drinks, but does so grudgingly; he feels immediate antipathy toward Weathers. This dislike is heightened by Weathers' ordering of expensive drinks (whiskey mixed with Appolinaris water) and by the entertainer's annoying refusal to reciprocate and buy drinks for the group of Irish men. It's important to remember that Farrington had to pawn his watch to pay for his desired alcohol; Weathers now takes advan-tage of him financially, only irritating him further.

This exchange also has political resonance, as once again the English element, represented by Weathers, exploits the poorer na-tion of Ireland, represented by Farrington, who can ill-afford such treatment. Indeed, when Weathers complains that their "hospital-ity was too Irish," he does so unconvincingly, since he willingly partakes of this generosity.

Finally, Farrington's drunken friends call upon him to "uphold the national honor" and arm wrestle with Weathers. The contest is seen jokingly as England versus Ireland, but once again, the politi-cal symbolism is profound. Weathers—thin and pallid—beats Farrington by cheating and Farrington feels humiliated at losing to "such a stripling." Time and again, the Irish of Joyce's time were defeated and humiliated by the British, often—Joyce believed—unfairly. Like the Irish, Farrington has no recourse and must suffer the sting of defeat, even though he has gone broke buying drinks for the man.

"Full of smoldering anger and revengefulness," Farrington re-turns home, still wanting to drink himself into a stupor to forget the two humiliations of his day. Even his wife, Joyce tells us, bullies—her husband whether he is drunk or sober. Like little Chandler, Farrington is trapped in an untenable life. When his son tells him Ada is at church, Farrington feels even more bereft of support and angry at his circumstances. Thus it shouldn't surprise the reader that Farrington lashes out at the only character in the story more helpless than he: his little boy.

As Farrington beats the child without reason, the boy falls to his knees in a manner of supplication and prayer, but even this won't deter his father from unleashing a full day's worth of anger upon him. The frightened boy begs him to stop, attempting to assuage his fury by offering to pray for him, but this appeal is meaningless to Farrington. In the face of degradation such as that which Farrington has endured, Joyce tells us, the contrivances of Irish Catholicism are useless, as ineffectual as the boy's helpless pleas for mercy.

Study Questions

1. What tone does Alleyne take when reprimanding Farrington?

2. Why does Joyce describe Alleyne as small and egg-shaped in appearance?

3. Where does Farrington imply that he's been going all afternoon?

4. What is suggested by the fact that Farrington holds out for an extra shilling (a small amount) at the pawnbroker's?

5. What is the symbolism implied in Farrington's pawning of his watch?

6. The bartender is referred to as a "curate." What's the irony in this?

7. What is the significance of the alluring woman at the bar?

8. Farrington's wife is at the chapel when he returns. What is the irony in this?

9. Why is Farrington so often referred to as "the man" instead of by name?

10. Why can't Farrington recognize which of his children approaches him at the end of the story?

Answers

1. He condescends to Farrington as if the latter were a child, implying Farrington's absolute powerlessness.

2. Alleyne is childlike in appearance, indicating that he, too, is powerless among his own level. None of these characters has meaningful control over his destiny.

3. He implies that he's been visiting the men's room, but it isn't believed.

4. It indicates how broke Farrington actually is.

5. The watch represents time and the future. However, he doesn't care about his future since he needs a drink so badly.

6. A "curate" is also a name for a priest. Farrington needs alcohol like others need religion.

7. She represents another element that Farrington can't have (like money or power). It's a further frustration for him.

8. Although she's religious, this can't salvage her terrible life with her husband.

9. He has no individual identity; he's just another unimportant clerk.

10. His children mean nothing to him. They, too, lack individual identities for him.

Suggested Essay Topics

1. Discuss the ultimate cost of Farrington's witty retort to his boss.

2. Draw the parallels between Little Chandler's circumstances and Farrington's. Why has Joyce juxtaposed their stories?

Clay

New Characters:

Maria: *middle-aged worker in an Irish charitable laundry*

Joe Donnelly: *her nephew*

Joe's Family

Summary

Maria, the protagonist in this story, works in a charitable laundry service in Dublin. This evening, Halloween, she has the night off after serving the laundresses their holiday cakes. On her way to visit her nephew Joe and his family, Maria carefully calculates how much she can spend on treats and picks up special desserts for Joe's family.

Once she arrives at their home, Maria discovers that she's left one of the costly treats in the tram and becomes upset at her absent-mindedness, but the family comforts her. Thereafter, the children play a holiday game in which the player is blindfolded and chooses between a number of objects laid out on a table. When Maria plays, she puts her hand in a mound of clay, which unsettles the family and upsets Joe's wife. The children re-arrange the objects and Maria chooses a prayer book on her second try.

Finally, Maria is asked to sing; she chooses an Irish ballad but mistakenly sings the first verse of the song twice. No one points out her error and her nephew's eyes fill with tears at the close of the ballad.

Analysis

Maria is a female celibate, a virgin, and her name calls to mind the Virgin Mary. Like a nun or a saint, Maria is a "veritable peacemaker," and her life revolves around the Dublin by Lamplight laundry. The laundry, according to Joyce's notes, was set up by a committee of Protestant society women to keep lower class girls and women off the streets of Dublin after dark. This presumably prevented them from theft or prostitution and engaged them in a useful chore instead. Maria functions as an ironic presence among

these bawdy women and brings cheer but is saintly rather than sinful, or even potentially sinful. Additionally, Maria is at peace with her Protestant employers; even though some of their traditions are strange to her, she finds them "very nice people." Her understanding, forgiveness, and kindness extend even to the drunk gentleman on the tram with whom Maria carries on a polite, restrained conversation.

Her life, however, is only half a life, Joyce indicates, because she has no intimate relationship, no sense of her physical self, and none of the longings of a mature adult. Playing the game of the barmbrack cakes on Halloween, Maria scoffs at the notion of finding the hidden ring (symbolizing love and marriage), telling Lizzie Flemming that "she didn't want any ring or man either." She finds her diminutive body "quaint" and "tidy," but Joyce never suggests Maria's womanliness; although she's clearly mature, it's unlikely that she's aware of this aspect of herself.

Buying cakes for her nephew, Maria blushes when asked (probably in jest) if she would like to buy a wedding cake, for the notion of an intimate union is completely foreign to her. This concept is furthered during the tram ride when, the author tells us, "none of the young men seemed to notice her" because her sexuality has been sublimated to the point of non-existence.

Joe's family delights in seeing Maria and receiving her gifts, but the first misstep of the evening is Maria's missing plum cake. Asking the children if they'd eaten it only annoys them, making the evening uncomfortable, and Maria feels disproportionately out of sorts by the loss, especially in light of its cost and the failure of her surprise.

The next embarrassment is the children's Halloween game of the saucers, wherein different items represent various life experiences: ring (romance, marriage); water (travel, adventure); prayer book (faith); clay (fear, death). Because of Maria's good works and faithful nature, the reader assumes she will choose the prayer book, but the children place the clay before her, to Maria's bewilderment and Mrs. Donnelly's vexation. It's clear, however, that Maria is afraid of life and is emotionally dead in her inability to form a close attachment. In this, she's similar to Eveline in the earlier story, though Maria's age and her lack of self-awareness lead us to believe that she will never even consider a change in her life. On her second try, Maria does indeed get the book, but the clay's negative implication colors the evening.

Finally, at her family's request, Maria sings "I Dreamt I Dwelt," an Irish song about love from the opera *The Bohemian Girl.* Her choice of song is ironic because Maria doesn't even dream about love (much less consider it a possibility). Furthermore, the "mistake" that her family doesn't point out is Maria's omission of the important second verse of the song which concerns being courted and loved by many suitors. Her omission symbolizes that Maria's consciousness cannot even contemplate a circumstance such as courtship, that she has obliterated this from her mind.

Maria believes her life full, but the minor upsets in the story become major losses to her because her life lacks any significant human (com)passion. She loves her nephew, but he cannot return the affection when drunk, as he often is, and his children seem alienated from her. Indeed, Maria seems alienated from the world due to her inability to see the emptiness in her life.

Study Questions

1. Joyce had originally intended to title this story "Hallowe'en." Why was the title changed to "Clay"?

2. To what degree is Maria able to develop a relationship at her job?

3. How does Maria's early relationship with her nephews compare to her present one?

4. What is the irony of Maria's description as a "peace-maker"?

5. Why is Joyce's description of Maria so grotesque?

6. Why, ironically, is Maria able to converse with the man on the train?

7. What is the significance of Joe's drinking problem?

8. How can we tell that Maria is alienated from Joe's children?

9. What is the ironic parallel between Maria visiting on Halloween and her description?

10. What is the significance of Maria's "mistake" in the song?

Answers

1. Clay is lifeless, like the meaningless relationships represented in this story.

2. She can develop no close relationships, since she works among Protestants (who do not share her religion) and lower class women (who do not share her lifestyle).

3. Although able to love them as children, Maria is too self-conscious to feel at ease with Joe now, and Alphy is far away.

4. The irony is that her two nephews no longer speak to one another, and it's impossible for Maria to make peace between them.

5. The degree to which she has lost her sexuality and sense of herself is so exaggerated that Maria is a grotesque (highly exaggerated and unrealistic) figure.

6. He's drunk, and therefore no meaningful conversation can take place.

7. Although Maria looks forward to a pleasant evening, she's obviously deluded about how enjoyable the experience actually is, since Joe needs to get drunk to enjoy it.

8. They immediately take offense when she asks them where the plumcake is.

9. Her witch-like physical appearance makes her an unwelcome visitor on Halloween, even though she's a deeply religious person.

10. It signifies her inability to conceptualize the idea of love—either romantic love or a non-romantic, but deep, connection to another person.

Suggested Essay Topics

1. How does Maria's attitude compare with Eveline's? Does either of the characters stand a chance at happiness?

2. Maria is a good person but not a balanced one. How (if at all) do her good intentions mitigate the degree to which her life is distorted?

A Painful Case

New Characters:

James Duffy: *middle-aged ascetic and scholar*

Emily Sinico: *middle-aged married woman who becomes attached to Duffy intellectually and personally*

Summary

James Duffy is a middle-aged ascetic who lives an isolated and intellectual life. He writes and reads philosophy, attends concerts, but lives far removed from human companionship.

At a concert, he meets Mrs. Emily Sinico, who attends the concert with her daughter. After she makes a comment, Duffy speaks to her. At their next chance meeting at another concert, he speaks more personally, finding out that her husband, a sea captain, often travels for long periods.

After their third accidental meeting, Duffy makes an appointment to see Mrs. Sinico, which then becomes routine. Fearing that he'll appear under-handed, he asks to be invited to Mrs. Sinico's home. Her husband encourages Duffy's visits for he thinks Duffy intends to ask for his daughter's hand in marriage.

In Emily, Duffy finds an intellectual companion with whom he can share books, discuss music and politics. Over time, the pair become more intimate until one evening, when Emily becomes so caught up in his conversation that she seizes Duffy's hand and presses it to her cheek. Duffy is repelled by her response and almost immediately breaks off his friendship with her.

Four years later, Duffy notices a news item in the paper stating that Mrs. Sinico was killed along a rail track in Dublin. Further in the article, Duffy notes comments from Emily's family that she had been acting strangely in recent years and also had begun drinking. Duffy is horrified that he had ever spoken to a person of Emily's temperament about his most intimate thoughts. Later, wandering around Dublin and considering her case, Duffy begins to second-guess himself about having broken off their relationship. Finally, he realizes that his withholding of a human connection with Emily had deprived him of companionship as well.

Analysis

In his memoir about his brother, Stanislaus Joyce states that this story was inspired by his own relationship with an older woman whom he met at a concert (159-160). The relationship ended without the bombast in this story, but James Duffy does share aspects of Stanislaus' character (the collecting of little quotations) as well of those of the author (the penchant for Nietzsche and the distrust of middle-class intellectuals).

Like Maria in "Clay," Duffy is a celibate leading an ascetic's life, and living "at a little distance from his body." Unlike her, Duffy enjoys no human intercourse. In fact, he avoids it; "visiting his relatives at Christmas and escorting them to the cemetery when they died" are his only obligations to others. Joyce is sarcastic in his description of Duffy's "spiritual" life, which has "neither companions nor friends, church nor creed," and no human communion whatsoever. One might well ask on what Duffy bases such "spirituality," but his own pompousness and condescension toward everyone else indicate that he worships only his own thoughts. That he composes short sentences about himself in the third person (i.e., "he") and in the past tense shows us even more strongly his alienation from his physical self.

Into his hermit's life wanders Emily Sinico, a lively, thoughtful woman whose husband "had dismissed his wife so sincerely from his gallery of pleasures that he did not suspect that anyone else would take an interest in her." Emily willingly, hungrily, shares Duffy's books, ideas, and intellectual life. Joyce tells us: "She listened to all." She becomes his spiritual sounding board, his "confessor," and Duffy revels in the audience she provides.

In Emily, Duffy senses someone who can reflect back to him his own glory. "He thought," Joyce tells us, "that in her eyes he would ascend to an angelical stature." Emily admires Duffy and attempts, futilely, to being him out of himself, to encourage him to enter the world. When she suggests that he publish his thoughts, he responds, "For what[?]" since he has no notion of what one gains from interaction with others. Nevertheless, their union wears away his resistance to another person, and he does begin to open emotionally to the woman. However, when Emily reaches out to him physically, Duffy is repulsed by the (presumed) intensity of her

gesture and afraid of the burden of her emotional needs. Almost immediately, he breaks off their friendship and returns to his former habits.

One evening, years later, he reads in shock that Mrs. Sinico has thrown herself before a moving train. His shock, however, isn't sadness but revulsion that he allowed himself to share his "sacred" thoughts with a woman he believes so obviously unbalanced. Duffy is so self-involved that he fails to grasp the woman's sense of loss and sadness, feeling instead that she had "deceived" him from seeing her true nature. Initially, he unquestioningly agrees with the paper's statement that attached "no blame" to anyone for the incident.

Wandering through the city streets and, ironically, ordering a "hot punch," Duffy begins to feel both his loss and his culpability. Emily was his confessor; he now has none. Moreover, he never sought out her feelings, never troubled himself to understand her obviously intense needs. Only her suicide awakens him to her life and its loneliness, but—he recognizes—this realization comes too late.

Similar to Henry James' John Marcher in "The Beast in the Jungle," Duffy recognizes he "withheld life" from the person most receptive to him and that he was now "an outcast from life's feast." At the story's end, he thinks he hears the sound of her name in the droning train engine, signifying his hope for some still-remote connection to her. However, this sound is illusory and, Joyce writes with finality, Duffy "felt that he was alone."

Study Questions

1. Mr. Duffy lives in Chapelizod, in legend associated with the great romance of Tristan and Isolde. Comment on the irony of this.

2. The reader is surprised to find a copy of Wordsworth's poetry on Duffy's shelf. Why?

3. Why is his liking for Mozart described as a dissipation?

4. Duffy collects quotations and communicates with Emily through them. What's the significance of this?

5. Why does Duffy insist that they meet at her house?

6. Why has it never occurred to Duffy to publish his ideas?

7. When he first learns of Emily's death, Duffy feels no responsibility. Why not?

8. Where does Duffy go to think about Emily, and why is this ironic?

9. Why does Joyce describe Duffy's reading of the obituary as in Secreto, like a priest?

10. Explain the significance of the very last word of the story.

Answers

1. It's ironic because Duffy is incapable of any love, let alone one as intense as that between Tristan and Isolde.

2. Wordsworth, probably one of the greatest Romantic poets of all time, expressed a desire to become more attuned to one's emotions through an understanding of one's environment and the natural world. Duffy is completely out of touch with his environment.

3. It is a dissipation in Duffy's eyes, not Joyce's. Duffy sees any enjoyment as somehow base.

4. It means he's unable to speak directly and honestly to her or express his own emotions.

5. He wants to meet there to avoid even the hint of underhanded behavior.

6. Publication implies a dialog with others, which involves a recognition of others. Duffy's has been previously incapable of this.

7. It's inconceivable to Duffy that he is responsible for the wellbeing of another human. This emphasizes how detached his life is.

8. He visits a secluded spot in Dublin called Magazine Hill. It's ironic because this is where lovers go to be alone with each other.

9. Duffy's celibate life has resembled a priest, but it's ironic because he has no spirituality.

10. Duffy is doomed to spend the rest of his life alone. It's too late for him to have "learned his lesson" and move on.

Suggested Essay Topics

1. Compare and contrast the life Maria is living (in "Clay") to that of James Duffy's.

2. After he learns of Emily's death, Duffy goes out and orders a "hot punch" (an alcoholic drink). Do you interpret this as a positive or negative sign about his ability to improve and change his life?

Ivy Day in the Committee Room

New Characters:

Old Jack: *caretaker of headquarters*

O'Connor: *young political canvasser*

Hynes: *canvasser whom others suspect of working for the rival side*

Henchy: a canvasser

Crofton: *a canvasser*

Lyons: *a canvasser*

Richard Tierney: *politician running for office in the Royal Exchange Ward and for whom the canvassers are working*

Father Keon: *de-frocked priest and friend of Tierney*

Charles Stewart Parnell: *(dead) Irish Revolutionary in whose honor ivy is worn on the lapel to commemorate anniversary of his death*

Summary

On the anniversary of the death of Irish political leader Charles Stewart Parnell, several political canvassers meet at headquarters

to compare progress and discuss an upcoming campaign. Although they all believe they're skilled pollsters and persuasive political manueverers, they are very cynical about their candidate, Richard Tierney, and the Dublin political process in general. They also fear that they might not be paid by Tierney; furthermore, he's even failed to deliver a complimentary case of Irish stout as promised.

As the canvassers converse with the caretaker of headquarters, other canvassers come and go, several checking to see if the money—or the stout—has been delivered. A de-frocked priest and friend of Tierney's, Father Keon, also appears but leaves almost immediately.

Finally, a boy delivers the stout to headquarters, and all of the canvassers partake of the alcohol, including the boy, whom they invite to drink before he departs. Suddenly, the canvassers are considerably more generous about Tierney than they first appeared, but another member discloses that he suspects one of the canvassers (Hynes) of betraying their campaign and working with a rival politician. They further question whether Edward VII is any more suitable a political leader than was Parnell during his lifetime, and the conversation switches to Parnell.

The group of canvassers becomes nostalgic for Parnell and prevails upon Hynes to recite a poem he had written on the death of the leader. After his reading, the group applauds.

Analysis

James Joyce was highly politicized as a child by his father, a fierce supporter of Irish nationalism and Charles Stewart Parnell, the leader of its cause at the time. When a love affair scandalized Parnell's name, he was ostracized by the very Irish masses who worshipped him and—in 1891—died after having been betrayed by many of his supporters. The concept of betrayal and Ireland's parochial and unforgiving stance toward Parnell, left a profound effect on the nine year-old James. These themes are a constant in his writing and very strong in this story, which takes place on the anniversary of Parnell's passing. To commemorate Parnell, the canvassers wear a sprig of ivy on their lapels.

Contradictions in this story abound, from the small and subtle to the large scale. O'Connor is described as a "grey-haired young

man" with a "husky falsetto" voice. Although all the men are can-
vassing votes for Richard Tierney, none likes him and all distrust
him, calling him "Tricky Dicky" and referring to his "little pig's eyes"
and unscrupulous character. In light of their distrust, it's ironic that
the men willingly campaign for him, promising one voter that "He's
a respectable man."

Ironies include their reversal of opinion about Tierney after
the politician sends the promised case of free alcohol to their headquarters. Before Tierney sends the complimentary stout, all the
men accuse him of miserly and unfair practices; everyone anticipates being cheated of wages. After the delivery, they decide that
Tierney is "not so bad after all. He's as good as his word, at least."
Clearly, a case of alcohol goes a long way in redeeming the sender's
character. This, too, gives evidence of the men's weak political commitment, their mercurial judge of character.

They delight in having the stout and drink it eagerly, offering a
bottle to the delivery boy as a tip. After he's gone, however, they
condemn the boy for under-age drinking, stating, "That's the way
it begins" in reference to alcoholism. Ironically, they notice the boy's
imagined problem but fail to scrutinize themselves.

Further hypocrisy is evidenced by the men's distrust of each
other in spite of the forced air of camaraderie. Henchy suspects
Hynes of double-crossing them with another candidate; Crofton
believes his colleagues are beneath him. Although they all wear
ivy to commemorate Parnell, several men strongly support King
Edward VII's visit to Ireland, a trip that Parnell himself protested in
1885. Finally, many of them are willing to overlook King Edward's
moral transgressions although Parnell, a hero, was shunned from
Irish politics for his. When Henchy asks, "Can't we Irish play fair?"
the answer, apparently, is no.

Given their confused morals and uncertain stance on politics,
fairness, and the betterment of Ireland, it's not surprising that the
caretaker, Old Jack, cannot keep a successful fire burning at headquarters. The fire—or passion—for a free and just Ireland has obviously gone out among these men. Twice O'Connor is asked by
another: "What are you doing in the dark?" The dark is literal and
figurative because all the men lack light and direction in their political consciences.

Despite the political atmosphere at headquarters, the one vibrant and respectable politician is, ironically, Parnell himself, whom Joyce believed could actually have saved Ireland. When Parnell's name arises, O'Connor vows "we all respect him now that he's dead and gone." Ironically, of course, their respect, the sprigs of ivy, and their false sentiment are meaningless to Parnell and Ireland "now that he's dead and gone." During the discussion of Parnell, the reader notices the corks flying out of the bottles of stout, which have been placed by the fire. Although the men are merely uncorking their alcohol, the repeated "Pok! Pok! Pok!" of the flying corks sarcastically resembles the military salute a fallen leader receives at a funeral. In Parnell's case, the pathetic uncorking of Irish stout is the best he receives from this gang of questionable campaigners, just as the shabby treatment of his political supporters was the best he received in his lifetime.

When the group becomes nostalgic for Parnell's day, when there was—Jack says—"some life in it then," they call upon Hynes to recite the poem he wrote to honor Parnell's passing. The poem praises Parnell as one of "Erin's heroes" and condemns the many who turned against him and tried to "smear the exalted name" of the politician. Ironically, the poet is the same man whom Henchy suspects of current political treachery, and many in the room—Joyce suggests—did nothing to save Parnell except make empty gestures. Hynes' poem closes by providing a hope that Parnell's political spirit may once more inspire Ireland to "rise like the Phoenix" to freedom. However, considering the ignoble and hypocritical state of Irish politics, this—Joyce believes—is an unlikely dream.

Study Questions

1. The men wear their collars turned up due to the weather. What is the irony in this?

2. Jack longs for the good old times of Ireland and Irish politics, but the younger men don't. What does this imply?

3. Before he was a politician, what was Richard Tierney's profession?

4. The men are extremely focused upon the arrival of the stout. What does this imply?

5. There's irony in their distrust of Tierney in light of question #4. What is it?

6. Why is Fr. Keon described as looking like "a poor clergyman or a poor actor"?

7. What does Tierney's connection with Keon imply?

8. What does O'Connor's unwillingness to discuss Parnell's history tell us?

9. What is the significance of all the contradictory elements in the story's narrative?

10. Comment on Crofton's response to Hyne's poem at the very end of the story.

Answers

1. The irony is that the ivy (which they wear in Parnell's honor) cannot be seen.

2. Jack, because he's older, has a greater sense of Parnell's significance, but the younger generation of Dublin politicians can't recognize this.

3. He ran a used clothing store, taking advantage of people and over-charging them.

4. It implies that they're alcoholics.

5. As soon as the stout arrives, their opinion of Tierney improves remarkably.

6. Keon is probably a de-frocked priest and not good at acting like one.

7. It implies that Tierney's background is questionable, like his friend Keon's.

8. It signifies a guilty conscience and an unwillingness to be honest about the past.

9. The men say they support what's best for Ireland, but they are—in fact—corrupt. They have no political consciences.

10. Crofton says "It's a fine piece of writing," but doesn't comment on the sentiment, which is its most important characteristic.

Suggested Essay Topics

1. What is ironic in Hyne's poem about the line: "For he lies dead whom the fell gang/Of modern hypocrites laid low"?

2. Comment on the last line of Hynes' poem in which he refers to the "One grief—the memory of Parnell." How does this relate to the characters in the story and their attitude(s)?

A Mother

New Characters:

Mrs. Kearney: *overbearing mother and socially ambitious member of Dublin middle class*

Mr. Kearney: *her quiet, ineffectual husband*

Kathleen Kearney: *her teenage daughter*

Mr. Holohan: *assistant secretary to the* Eire Abu *Society*

Mr. Fitzpatrick: *secretary to the* Eire Abu *Society*

Summary

Mrs. Kearney, a socially ambitious middle-class mother, arranges for her daughter Kathleen to play the piano at a fairly prestigious Celtic revival festival in Dublin. In order for the several performances to turn out splendidly, Mrs. Kearney spends extra money on the daughter's clothes, arranges the program, and orders several tickets for acquaintances. The arranger of the festival and assistant secretary to the society, Mr. Holohan, is so hapless in this planning stage that he accepts Mrs. Kearney's help gladly.

When the first two concerts arrive, Mrs. Kearney nervously observes that the house is nearly empty and the program poorly run. When told that the third and penultimate concert will be cancelled to guarantee a fuller house on the last night, Mrs. Kearney underscores to the society's secretary, Mr. Fitzpatrick, that this should not alter her daughter's contracted fee. Fitzpatrick is non-committal.

On the evening of the final night, Mrs. Kearney once again attempts to confirm that Kathleen will receive her promised sum.

When Fitzpatrick pays her four shillings short and doesn't discuss the remainder, Mrs. Kearney informs him that Kathleen will not play—even though the program has already commenced and the performers need an accompanist. Furious that her daughter's contract is of so little importance, Mrs. Kearney stubbornly insists, refusing to compromise, although such behavior attributed to the girl could ruin her future in Dublin music circles. Ultimately, Fitzpatrick, Holohan and Mrs. Kearney part, both sides furious with the other, and Kathleen having had no say in her own participation in the event.

Analysis

The surface incidents in "A Mother" portray Mrs. Kearney as an overbearing stage mother, and, to a degree, she certainly is. However, like the previous story, "A Mother" has political meaning which transcends this plot.

Because her daughter's name is Kathleen (the traditional name and personification of Ireland), Mrs. Kearney "takes advantage of her daughter's name" and involves her in the Gaelic revival movement popular among the Dublin middle class at the time. According to the author, this consists merely of learning Gaelic phrases and sending "Irish picture postcards" back and forth to friends; neither Kathleen nor her mother is genuinely politicized. Thus, Mrs. Kearney sees the invitation from the *Eire Abu* society (a patriotic society whose Gaelic name means "Ireland to victory!") as the perfect opportunity to showcase Kathleen's talents and culture. That the society hopes to generate support for and interest in native Irish culture doesn't seem significant to Mrs. Kearney, but she throws herself into its planning to guarantee a good audience for her daughter's debut. Taking over almost completely for Mr. Holohan, Mrs. Kearney arranges the program, buys tickets in advance, and provides for Kathleen's expensive gown.

Therefore, it stuns her to see the near-empty house on the festival's first night, a clear indicator of Dublin's lack of interest in things Gaelic. Further, Mrs. Kearney feels a growing frustration with Messrs. Fitzpatrick and Holohan (the secretary and assistant secretary of the society) who laconically accept the poor planning, bad attendance, and mediocre artistic performances.

Mrs. Kearney's annoyance and the men's inertia exemplify Joyce's impression of the Irish political movement: troubled from within by divergent goals and personalities, thwarted from success by inept management. Although there's obviously a problem in the concert's planning, only Mrs. Kearney notices it; the others are too involved in the importance of their own roles to focus on the larger good. Additionally, Mrs. Kearney is not a director although she at times behaves like one; as a woman, she has no power to command attention or run the operation. Ironically, her husband, by virtue of his "abstract value as a man" could exercise some authority but is too weak and passive to do so. As a result, the concert, like the Irish political movement itself, is a chaotic mess.

When the society secretaries intimate that Kathleen Kearney's contract won't be honored in full, Mrs. Kearney justifiably feels her efforts taken for granted and her daughter exploited. The society, however, fails to grasp the injustice, simply seeing it as a result of the concert's poor attendance. This also symbolizes Ireland's dilemma, as the failure of the cause punishes members who have expended a great deal in return for its failure. "We did our best," shrugs a woman backstage, but this doesn't comfort Mrs. Kearney who feels bitter about the failure and subsequent deception.

Stubbornly, she insists upon the contract, even when the management offers a lukewarm compromise. Other performers choose sides between the two groups, and the scene backstage resembles a battlefield—or a boxing match—with each warring faction and its supporters in a separate corner.

Due to the conflict, a character remarks, "Kathleen Kearney's musical career was ended in Dublin." As an additional affront, Miss Healy, a great friend of Kathleen, agrees to substitute for her, effectively wiping Kathleen's musical future away. Mrs. Kearney takes no heed of the controversy's deleterious effects on Kathleen or her future. The society, itself dedicated to Ireland's victory, feels no unease about swindling a young member. Because of the warring from within, Gaelic culture isn't celebrated successfully and the union breaks down completely. This poorly managed and bitter experience, Joyce implies, is the future of Irish nationalism, washed up by mutual stubbornness, pettiness, and self-absorption.

Study Questions

1. What is the significance of Mr. Holohan's limp?

2. Why is Mrs. Kearney so overbearing and eager to showcase her daughter at any cost?

3. Explain the similarity between Mr. Holohan and Mr. Kearney.

4. The story's controversy centers around Kathleen Kearney's playing, but she never speaks. What the implication of this?

5. Madam Glynn, the English soprano, is described as "startled" and "meagre." What does she represent?

6. What is ironic about the *Eire Abu* society?

7. What is Joyce's implication in the poor quality of the performances artistes?

8. The name Healy was notorious in Joyce's day because it was the name of one of Charles Parnell's most famous political betrayers. What is the significance of Miss Healy's name in this story?

9. What is the significance of the two groups of Irish fighting at a festival for Irish culture?

10. What is the significance of the "threats" at the story's end?

Answers

1. It implies his ineffectiveness and incapacity; he symbolizes the Irish independence movement's impotency.

2. She hopes to make her daughter a star in society.

3. They are both ineffective and weak men; therefore, Mrs. Kearney can manipulate them.

4. It implies that she's as domineered by her mother as her father is; she's merely a pawn or instrument or her mother's ambition.

5. She represents the negative influence British culture has on Ireland's culture. Her presence adds nothing to the event.

6. Their name means "Ireland to Victory," so it's ironic that they can't even successfully put on a talent show. This is Joyce's

     sarcastic comment about ineffectual organizations that can't approach Irish nationalism meaningfully.

7.   He implies that their talents in the performing arts are akin to their "talents" as participants in Ireland's independence.

8.   When Kathleen refuses to perform out of principle, Miss Healy takes her place. Healy's playing is a betrayal of her "great friend," as was the case with Parnell.

9.   It symbolizes the Irish conflict between Protestants (in the north) and Catholics (primarily in the south).

10. The threats are ambiguous and imply an unresolved conflict, just as the tension between the Irish (and with Britain) remained unresolved and bitter.

Suggested Essay Topics

1.   Compare and contrast Mrs. Kearney and her situation to Mrs. Mooney ("The Boarding House") and hers.

2.   Comment on the role Irish culture does (or does not) play in this story.

Grace

New Characters:

Tom Kernan: *a tea merchant and alcoholic*

Messrs. Power, Cunningham, M'Coy and Fogarty—*Tom Kernan's friends*

Mrs. Kernan—*his wife*

Father Purdon—*priest running the "businessman's retreat" at the local church*

Summary

    The beginning of "Grace" finds Tom Kernan, a tea merchant, lying face-down and drunk on the lavatory floor of a Dublin pub. Helpless and incoherent, Kernan is saved from further embarrassment by his friend, Mr. Power, who delivers him home to his wife.

Two days later, Kernan receives three visitors: Messrs. Power, Cunningham, and M'Coy. Unbeknownst to Kernan, Power has informed Mrs. Kernan that the three friends intend to bring Tom to a church retreat that will help him mend his ways. The three shrewdly suggest that Kernan join and he agrees, believing it was his idea—and not theirs—that he come along.

The retreat has been specifically designed for businessmen, and the four friends are joined by a fifth, the grocer Fogarty, and many other merchants whom they know from the community. The priest, Father Purdon, delivers a sermon on a passage from the Gospel of Luke (16:8-9), which he tells them is designed for men who live "in the world and, to a certain extent, for the world." The men listen attentively.

Analysis

Stanislaus Joyce tells us that his brother patterned Tom Kernan's progress in this story after Dante's *Divine Comedy*: the "fall down the steps of the lavatory is his descent into hell, the sickroom is purgatory, and the Church [...] is paradise at last" (228). Of course, a close reading shows us that Kernan and his friends will never reach paradise, as they really have no clear concept of the soul, penance, or the divine act of Grace itself. This sarcastic comparison to Dante is the basis for Joyce's story: he felt too many Irish Catholics believed in a lazy, spiritually devoid religion that Kernan's group represents. According to his brother, Joyce attended a sermon on Grace at the same Gardiner Street church referred to in the story, and returned "angry and disgusted" at the distorted exposition he heard. Because it so infuriated him that "such shoddy stuff should pass for spiritual guidance," Stanislaus writes, the concept behind the story was born (227).

Ironically, Tom Kernan is a tea-taster by profession, but it is whiskey—not tea—that has caused him to careen down the stairs of a men's room in a drunken stupor. Having bitten off the end of his tongue as well, Kernan can't even express himself until the young cyclist and Kernan's friend, Power, rescue him.

As he recuperates, Kernan is visited by three of his friends: Power Cunningham, and M'Coy. Joyce intentionally assembles three visitors to construct a mock trinity, not the holy trinity in the

Christian sense. In fact, the friends, representing (with their alle-
gorical names) power and cunning, have come to make Kernan
"the victim of a plot" intended, ironically, to save his soul.

As the men speak of the Church and Catholicism, the sub-
stance of their discussion tells us a great deal about their potential
for Grace and salvation. For example, although he provides them
with a seemingly endless supply of information about Christianity, the Pope and Church doctrine, Martin Cunningham's recollection of "facts" and "history" is completely erroneous. Joyce tells us
his words "built up the vast image of the Church in the minds of
his hearers"; however, virtually all of Cunningham's statements are
a mixture of mistakes, lies, and general misinformation. Since his
friends are equally ignorant about the Church, they accept his statements unquestioningly and even admiringly.

In the matter of faith and redemption, the men are equally
inadequate, seeing Tom's salvation as "a little...spiritual matter"
and comparing his participation at the retreat to "a four-handed
reel." (emphasis added) The characters' use of slang to discuss
spiritual issues, such as Cunningham's suggestion that they "wash
the pot" together, further indicates their inability to recognize the
act of contrition as a serious matter. Indeed, the retreat itself—traditionally a time of contemplation and atonement—is described
by Cunningham as "just a kind of friendly talk, you know, in a com-
mon-sense way." Joyce knew from his Jesuit training that spiritual
Grace and redemption were profound and mysterious, not to be
approached through "common sense" with a priest who "won't be
too hard" on his listeners.

As the men drink whiskey to celebrate their renewed vow of
piety, Cunningham inadvertently pronounces Joyce's judgment of
such Catholics: "we may as well admit we're a nice collection of
scoundrels."

Inside the Gardiner Street church where the retreat is set, Joyce
describes the men, joined by Mr. Fogarty, as "well dressed and or-
derly" with their hats carefully resting upon their knees. Although
they look respectable, the assembled group is indeed a "collection
of scoundrels": a money-lender, a political dealer and "mayor-
maker," a pawnshop owner, and others with similarly questionable backgrounds. Among this group, the alcoholic Kernan "began

to feel more at home" since he's surrounded by unrepentant sinners like himself.

Father Purdon (whose name reminds us of "pardon") preaches on the parable of the unjust steward from Luke, but his reading of this excerpt contorts its biblical meaning for the convenience and complacency of his listeners. Contrary to Purdon's statement, it's unlikely that the parable was specifically designed to guide "business men and professional men" in their worldly affairs. Because Purdon is also "a man of the world" and not a man of God, he simplifies the complex workings of Grace and faith, telling the men misleadingly that "Jesus Christ was not a hard task master." The goals of their retreat, he adds, are neither "terrifying" nor "extravagant." The irony, of course, is this: were the men actually able to discern the degenerate state of their souls (as the readers are), they would be terrified to grasp the extent of their corruption.

As the deluded men and the unscrupulous priest approach the mystery of Grace "in a businesslike way," we understand that their redemption is impossible, for spirituality is *not* business. The laziness and misguidedness of this self-deceiving group will forever prevent them from adequately examining the state of their consciences. In effect, Joyce hopes that his story acts as a parable to shake the reader out of a similar complacency.

Study Questions

1. Considering the title, why is Kernan's fall ironic?

2. Comment on the meaning of grace in the following quote: "[Kernan] had never been seen in the city without a silk hat of some decency and a pair of gaiters. By grace of these two articles of clothing, he said, a man could always pass muster."

3. Why is it ironic that Mrs. Kernan celebrated her anniversary by waltzing with her husband "to Mr. Power's accompaniment"?

4. What is significant about Mr. M'Coy's comment that the Jesuits are "the boyos [that] have influence"?

5. When Kernan recollects hearing Fr. Tom Burke preach, he recalls that he sat in "back near the door." What does this symbolize?

6. Mr. Kernan refers to the lighting of a sacramental candle as "the magic-lantern business." What does his attitude tell us about his belief?

7. What is the symbolism of the "distant speck of red light" in the Gardiner Street church?

8. Why does Purdon appear to be "struggling up" to the pulpit for his sermon?

9. Why does Joyce tell us the priest covers his face with hands when he prays towards the light?

10. What is ironic about the concept of a priest acing as a "spiritual accountant" for these men?

Answers

1. In the sense that grace connotes "graceful," Kernan stumbles because he's drunk. He lacks grace of the spiritual or physical kind.

2. For Kernan, his friends, and even Fr. Purdon, grace is seen as something superficial. Kernan believes that if he looks presentable on the surface, he can "pass muster."

3. Even though Kernan has not been a good husband, Power is determined to keep the couple together; he acts as their bond.

4. All of the men consider spirituality a "business" matter, so it's ironic and humorous that M'Coy would talk about priests as having "influence" with God!

5. Kernan was unable to actually approach the idea of salvation; his sitting near the door implies his figurative and literal distance from God.

6. Jesus said that he was the light of the world, but Kernan does not want to partake of the lighting ritual. This indicates his lack of commitment to the matter of salvation.

7. The red light in a church indicates the presence of the Blessed Sacrament. In this church, with these listeners, the sacrament is very "distant."

8. He struggles because he is a corrupt priest who doesn't belong in the pulpit.

9. His covering his face indicates his unworthiness to preach and lead a congregation. He's unable to face the light of the Sacrament.

10. These men are so materialistic and unspiritual that they can only think in terms of money and accounts. It's ironic and pathetic that they even think in terms of their souls as account ledgers.

Suggested Essay Topics

1. Compare and contrast the figure of the priest in "The Sisters" and in "Grace."

2. Discuss the use of irony as it applies to all the men in this story. (Kernan's friends, the priest, and Kernan himself)

The Dead

New Characters:

Gabriel Conroy: *teacher and amateur writer*

Gretta Conroy: *his wife*

Julia and Kate Morkan: *Gabriel's aging aunts, piano and voice teachers in Dublin*

Mary Jane: *Gabriel's cousin, an unmarried piano teacher who lives with the aunts*

Molly Ivors: *Gabriel's colleague and passionate Irish nationalist various party guests of the Morkans*

Michael Furey: *(dead) adolescent love of Gretta Conroy*

Summary

At the opening of "The Dead," Gabriel Conroy, a teacher and amateur writer, arrives with his wife, Gretta, at a Christmas party given by his aunts, Julia and Kate Morkan. Though the mood of the

annual affair is festive, Gabriel is unnerved by a series of misunder-
standings and uncomfortable events during the evening. In chat-
ting with the maid, Gabriel makes a slight *faux pas* to which she
answers bitterly. Later, dancing with a colleague from school, Gabriel
argues with her about Irish nationalism and her response offends
him. Finally, in making a toast to the evening's hostesses, Gabriel
agonizes over what to say—and second-guesses himself for the rest
of the evening about whether his choice was appropriate.

When the time comes to leave for the hotel at which they're
staying, Gabriel finds his wife listening to a tenor singing an Irish
ballad in the music room, and his thoughts about Gretta turn amo-
rous. On the way home in the cab, Gabriel anticipates a night of
passion but waits until the moment they're alone to approach her.
Gretta, on the other hand, seems distracted and tired, which annoys him. When he finally does approach her, Gretta stuns her
husband by telling him about a country boy, Michael Furey, whom
she loved years ago and who died at 17.

After Gretta cries herself to sleep, Gabriel considers this new
knowledge about his wife, pondering what it says about his life and
his identity. As snow begins to fall, Gabriel imagines he sees Michael
Furey outside the window, and then considers his own mortality
and the irrevocability of death that awaits everyone.

Analysis

According to a letter Joyce sent to his brother in 1905, he had
crafted the *Dubliners* stories into groups representing childhood,
adolescence, maturity, and Dublin's private life (Ellmann, *James
Joyce*, 208). "The Dead" could easily be placed in either of the last
two categories. However, this story was added later, in 1907, after
Joyce had seen—and become disillusioned with—other cities in
Europe. Therefore, his original intention to paint a gritty and un-
flattering portrait of his native city in *Dubliners* was somewhat
mellowed by the time he approached this narrative. As a result,
while the story contains similar themes of paralysis and spiritual
moribundity that the other stories share, Joyce's treatment of the
characters and issues is slightly less caustic and more merciful than
in the previous pieces.

Gabriel Conroy, the story's protagonist, bears the name of the archangel Gabriel who brought news of the births of both John the Baptist and the Messiah to the world. However, each message that Gabriel conveys and encounters in this story has a disappointing and sometimes unsettling result for him. His small talk with Lily the maid brings up the subject of young suitors and annoys her thoroughly. While recovering from her bitter retort, Gabriel begins to agonize over the toast he'll give later to his aging aunts, Julia and Kate Morkan. Though the party and hostesses are full of warmth and good cheer, Gabriel is distracted by the inadequacy and inappropriateness of the message, since the party-goers' "grade of culture differed from his." Intellectually, Gabriel is a snob who consciously detaches himself from his acquaintances and friends. Yet his self-confidence is as low as his anxiety is high, and he worries that his toast "would fail with them just as he had failed with the girl in the pantry."

Although named after a celestial messenger, Gabriel cannot express himself clearly and honestly; part of his frustration comes from an inability (seen so often in *Dubliners*) to understand and express his emotions, to reach out to another in genuine communion.

While dancing with Molly Ivors, Gabriel is interrogated about the extent of his patriotic feelings, since Molly is an ardent nationalist. Progressively, Molly's questions become more accusatory, demanding to know why he doesn't embrace his native country and native language (Gaelic). Gabriel can neither defuse the conversation nor provide a suitable response, exploding suddenly: "I'm sick of my own country, sick of it!" As a final launch against his beliefs (or lack thereof), Molly whispers in Gabriel's ear "West Briton!" implying that he is an Anglicized Irishman, and effectively destroying his mood for the rest of the evening.

Hoping for succor from his wife, Gabriel tells Gretta about Molly's plan to visit western Ireland, but—rather than support Gabriel's decision—Gretta jumps for joy at the thought of re-visiting her childhood home and is summarily denied. For Gabriel, the tension between the western and eastern sections of the country represents his discomfort with his Irishness and his own personality. Investigating the western part of Ireland or Irish traditions, Joyce suggests, would force Gabriel to confront a different side of

himself, a more emotional side. Allusions to the west, which abound here and towards the end of the story, are potentially threatening to him. For example, Gabriel shows offense when Molly reminds him that his wife is from Connacht (in the west) and still resents his dead mother for once deeming Gretta too countrified.

Joyce implies that the rural, western section of the country (his own wife's birthplace) was emotionally freer, more authentic, less repressed and distorted by its proximity to England and the continent whose influences bastardized Irish culture. Gabriel, however, feels uncomfortable with the openness of feeling this implies, just as he's uncomfortable with Molly's blunt questioning and his wife's rural background. Indeed, Gabriel feels much more at home with English and European influences rather than those of Ireland. For example, he considers quoting Browning (an English poet) in his toast, prefers vacations in France, Belgium, or Germany, and even introduces his family to the habit of wearing galoshes, telling Aunt Julia "everyone wears them on the continent."

The toast Gabriel strains over, however, does genuinely praise the Irish tradition of hospitality which Joyce felt was unmatched throughout Europe. The carefully described dinner scene—with its table-load of delicacies—emphasizes this tradition that the Morkans represent—traditions that, unfortunately, may die out with their generation. Ironically, Gabriel praises these traditional Irish qualities and recognizes them even while regarding his aunts as "two ignorant old women." A further irony is Gabriel's criticism of the "new generation" of "hyper-educated," "thought-tormented" intellectuals, since Gabriel considers himself an intellectual, and overly-educated for his milieu. This comment in the toast could also reflect Joyce's feelings about himself and fellow intellectuals, whose detached view of the world might have sometimes compromised their emotional vibrancy.

The dinner conversation about the late-great opera singers further illustrates Joyce's theme that the magnificence of the past is fading, if not gone completely. It also reflects Dublin's glorious past but now uncertain future, because many of the "good singers" no longer choose to perform there, preferring instead the cities on the continent. Finally, the story of the dead opera heroes, the monks who sleep in their coffins, and Patrick Morkan's deceased horse all highlight the topic of death, returning us to the title and theme of the story. The greatness they admire (be it in opera singers or Ireland's cultural past) lies in the past with the dead. The living, the author suggests, are doomed to remember and long for it, but they cannot rekindle it, as many of these scenes reflect.

The most stunning recollection of the past is Gretta's admission that she was passionately loved by a teenager, Michael Furey, when she was a girl in western Ireland. Listening to the simple Irish ballad "The Lass of Aughrim" reminds Gretta of his profound love, and Michael suddenly becomes more vivid an experience for her than those in her present life. Ironically, Michael (whose last name reminds us of "fury" or "passion") brings about a more impassioned reaction in her than her own husband does, even though Gabriel had deeply passionate fantasies about Gretta as they rode to the hotel.

Although this discovery makes him jealous and irritable at first, Gabriel dwells on thoughts of Michael Furey long into the night, after Gretta has fallen asleep. For the first time in the story, Gabriel abandons his own self-consciousness and narcissism to sympathize with Gretta and empathize with Michael, as "[g]enerous tears fill his eyes." Confronting Gretta's private emotions for the first time, Gabriel is able to understand the quality of her earlier love; though he doesn't possess the capacity for such passion, he recognizes its importance. In a delusionary vision, Gabriel imagines that he sees the figure of Michael Furey standing under a tree outside his window. This signifies the degree to which Gabriel is able to share his wife's emotion (and loss), as his soul "approache[s]" that region where dwell the vast hosts of the dead."

Gabriel is devastated by Gretta's disclosure, but the emotional epiphany it inspires allows him to reach a more profound understanding of his world than he has yet evidenced in the story. His empathy for Gretta, his elderly aunts, and even Michael Furey suggests that he may have broken through his previous emotional paralysis.

The snow falling "all over Ireland" is a double signifier at the end of Gabriel's reverie. Snow, obviously, is frozen and connotes things "frozen in place"; this indicates that Gabriel's awakening and

the state of his marriage may not develop a great deal more than they have already. Likewise, the people in his world long for earlier times and repeat the same customs and traditions, regardless of their intrinsic value; there is little forward movement or evolution. On the other hand, the snow is "general," falling, Joyce tells us, "upon all the living and the dead" and suggesting a kind of commonality or kinship between past and present. As Richard Ellmann suggests, the snow implies "mutuality" among men, "a sense of their connection with each other, a sense that none has his being alone" ("Backgrounds of 'The Dead,'" 399). If Gabriel senses this even unconsciously, he can at least begin to recognize his emotional isolation, and this—Joyce suggests—is the key to remediating the spiritual and emotional paralysis that plagues his Dubliners.

Study Questions

1. What function does the "fringe of snow" on Gabriel's coat play at the story's beginning?

2. When Mary Jane plays the piano, "the only persons who seemed to follow the music was Mary Jane herself." What does this signify?

3. Why is it ironic that Molly Ivors and Gabriel dance to an Irish tune during their argument?

4. During the argument, Gabriel "wanted to say that literature was above politics," but he doesn't. What is Joyce's opinion about that belief?

5. What is signified by the fact that Gabriel—standing in the party—longs to "walk out alone, first along the river and then through the park"?

6. What is ironic about Aunt Julia's choice of song for the guests: "Arrayed for the Bridal"?

7. Why does Gabriel's mood suddenly lift right before dinner?

8. Gabriel's toast to "the past, of youth, […] of absent faces" is ironic in light of Gretta's later revelation, why?

9. Gabriel gazes at his wife who stands in "a dark part of the hall." What does this tell us about his relationship to her?

10. What is the "impalpable and vindictive being" that overtakes Gabriel when he learns that Michael Furey may have died for love of Gretta?

Answers

1. It foreshadows the importance of the snow imagery at the end of the story.

2. It signifies the sterile and emotionless quality that complex art has for its viewers and listeners. Joyce wants us to compare this to the moving performances of the Irish folk ballads further on in the story.

3. It's ironic because they are arguing about the value of Irish culture while dancing to an Irish song.

4. Joyce believed that politics and literature were intimately and indelibly linked.

5. It speaks of Gabriel's emotional isolation.

6. Wearing dark clothes, with her sunken grey face and distracted air, Aunt Julia is the antithesis of a bridal image and more closely represents death in her appearance and manner.

7. He discovers that Molly Ivors has left and blames her for his foul mood.

8. Because Gretta will soon be distracted by thoughts of her past youth and the absent, haunting face of Michael Furey.

9. Gabriel is "in the dark" about his wife's emotional life, although later he longs to "be the master of her strange mood."

10. It is the force of the dead.

Suggested Essay Topics

1. How does Gabriel's inadequacy and discomfort with his surroundings compare and contrast with that of James Duffy's ("A Painful Case")?

2. Gabriel longs to write, think, and even paint expressively, reminding us of Little Chandler ("A Little Cloud"). How are the two similar? Different?

3. Discuss the many ironies presented in Gabriel's toast to his two aunts and cousin.

4. Compare the circumstances of Gabriel's life and aspirations to those of Little Chandler in "A Little Cloud."

Sample Analytical Paper Topics

Topic #1

Discuss three instances in the collection wherein a dead or missing figure possesses greater vitality than do those of the present. Indicate the influence these dead have on the living who remember them.

Outline

I. Thesis Statement: *Whether a deceased relative, former love, or prominent political figure, the figures of the dead in* Dubliners *influence the lives and behavior of the living to a profound degree. Of particular significance are the dead characters haunting the characters in "Eveline," "Ivy Day," and "The Dead."*

II. Eveline

    A. Mother

        1. Keeps Eveline from moving away from home.

        2. Continues to induce guilt that makes her subservient to her father.

    B. Brother Ernest

        1. Happy memories of childhood fool Eveline into thinking her current family life is bearable.

III. Ivy Day in the Committee Room

    A.   Charles Stewart Parnell

        1.   Reminds the political canvassers of their unfair treatment of him years earlier.

        2.   Unsettles their consciences regarding their current political practices.

        3.   Inspires in some a desire to be truer to the cause of Irish autonomy.

IV.   The Dead

    A.   Gabriel's Mother

        1.   In guaranteeing Gabriel a superior education, also made him overly conscious of his intellectual superiority, thereby stifling the emotional side of his character.

        2.   Always disregarded Gretta as being beneath her son because Gretta was a country girl.

    B.   Michael Furey

        1.   Causes Gretta anguish as she remembers that she was partly responsible for his death.

        2.   Reminds Gretta of the emotional void she currently has in relationship with Gabriel.

Topic #2

Discuss the inequities of class and gender in three stories and the consequences of these inequities.

Outline:

I.   Thesis Statement: *Gender and class cause certain members of Dublin society to be oppressed by others, often forcing them to submit to humiliation, degradation and—to some degree—the selling of their self-worth. In these same stories, those in a "superior" position exploit those beneath them to help support their own fragile existence.*

II.   Two Gallants

    A.   Corley treats servant girls abusively because he is from a higher class.

    B.   The girls Corley mistreats endure his boorishness in hopes that he'll marry them.

III. The Boarding House

    A.   Mrs. Mooney allows her daughter to compromise her values in order to "trap" a husband.

    B.   Because he needs to hold onto his job, Bob Doran allows himself to be forced into an undesirable marriage.

    C.   Because an unmarried woman had no way of providing for herself, Polly Mooney must accept Doran as a husband, even though they are incompatible.

IV. Counterparts

    A.   Farrington must endure being verbally abused by his boss because he probably could not find other employment.

    B.   Farrington's wife cannot expect support from him but cannot leave him because:

        1.   She's Catholic.

        2.   She has five children to support and would be unable to earn wages on her own.

    C.   Farrington's son Tom must bear the brunt of his father's anger because he's too young and helpless to live on his own.

Topic #3

    Discuss the theme of the "unlived life" as it's represented in at least three of the stories.

Outline

I.   Thesis Statement: *Due to their spiritual paralysis, many of Joyce's characters cannot seize the opportunities they long for, even when such opportunity is close within their grasp. Fear, self-doubt and psychic inertia have caused these characters to halt the progress of their own development, abandoning any possibility of or hope for change.*

II. A Little Cloud

    A. Little can't become a poet because he's too afraid to take a risk in his life.

    B. Intimidated by his wife, whom he doesn't love, Little must obey her.

    C. Because of his frustration and lack of emotional fulfillment, Little cannot enjoy (or love) his own son.

III. Clay

    A. Maria works in an artificially sheltered environment around people with whom she doesn't enjoy an emotional connection.

    B. Afraid of her sexuality and/or maturity, Maria lives a celibate life.

    C. Because her existence is so devoid of substantial meaning, Maria's life revolves around trivialities which frustrate and sometimes bewilder her.

IV. A Painful Case

    A. Duffy has convinced himself that he needs no human contact and has robbed himself of emotional interaction.

    B. Emily Sinico has been deprived of human affection by her husband.

    C. Because of each of their thwarted experience in relationships with others, neither character can successfully reach out to the other.

    D. As a result, both destroy themselves:

        1. Emily by suicide.

        2. Duffy by self-deception and, therefore, a missed opportunity for love.

Bibliography

Quotations from *Dubliners* are taken from the following edition:

Joyce, James. *Dubliners.* (1916) Eds. Robert Scholes and A. Walton Litz. New York: The Viking Press, 1982.

Other Sources:

Brandabur, Edward. "The Sisters." *Dubliners.* eds. Robert Scholes and A. Walton Litz. New York: The Viking Press, 1982. 333-343.

Ellmann, Richard. "The Backgrounds of 'The Dead.'" Dubliners. eds. Robert Scholes and A. Walton Litz. New York: The Viking Press, 1982. 388-403.

_____. *James Joyce.* New York: The Viking Press, 1975.

_____. ed. *Selected Letters of James Joyce.* New York: The Viking Press, 1975.

Joyce, Stanislaus. *My Brother's Keeper: James Joyce's Early Years.* New York: The Viking Press, 1958.

Litz, A. Walton. "Two Gallants." *Dubliners.* eds. Robert Scholes and A. Walton Litz. New York: The Viking Press, 1982. 368-387.

Stone, Harry. "'Araby' and the Writings of James Joyce." *Dubliners.* eds. Robert Scholes and A. Walton Litz. New York: The Viking Press, 1982. 344-367.

MAXnotes

REA's Literature Study Guides

MAXnotes® are student-friendly. They offer a fresh look at masterpieces of literature, presented in a lively and interesting fashion. **MAXnotes**® offer the essentials of what you should know about the work, including outlines, explanations and discussions of the plot, character lists, analyses, and historical context. **MAXnotes**® are designed to help you think independently about literary works by raising various issues and thought-provoking ideas and questions. Written by literary experts who currently teach the subject, **MAXnotes**® enhance your understanding and enjoyment of the work.

Available **MAXnotes**® include the following:

Absalom, Absalom!	Heart of Darkness	Of Mice and Men
The Aeneid of Virgil	Henry IV, Part I	On the Road
Animal Farm	Henry V	Othello
Antony and Cleopatra	The House on Mango Street	Paradise Lost
As I Lay Dying	Huckleberry Finn	A Passage to India
As You Like It	I Know Why the Caged	Plato's Republic
The Autobiography of	Bird Sings	Portrait of a Lady
Malcolm X	The Iliad	A Portrait of the Artist
The Awakening	Invisible Man	as a Young Man
Beloved	Jane Eyre	Pride and Prejudice
Beowulf	Jazz	A Raisin in the Sun
Billy Budd	The Joy Luck Club	Richard II
The Bluest Eye, A Novel	Jude the Obscure	Romeo and Juliet
Brave New World	Julius Caesar	The Scarlet Letter
The Canterbury Tales	King Lear	Sir Gawain and the
The Catcher in the Rye	Les Misérables	Green Knight
The Color Purple	Lord of the Flies	Slaughterhouse-Five
The Crucible	Macbeth	Song of Solomon
Death in Venice	The Merchant of Venice	The Sound and the Fury
Death of a Salesman	The Metamorphoses of Ovid	The Stranger
The Divine Comedy I: Inferno	The Metamorphosis	The Sun Also Rises
Dubliners	Middlemarch	A Tale of Two Cities
Emma	A Midsummer Night's Dream	Taming of the Shrew
Euripedes' Electra & Medea	Moby-Dick	The Tempest
Frankenstein	Moll Flanders	Tess of the D'Urbervilles
Gone with the Wind	Mrs. Dalloway	Their Eyes Were Watching God
The Grapes of Wrath	Much Ado About Nothing	To Kill a Mockingbird
Great Expectations	My Antonia	To the Lighthouse
The Great Gatsby	Native Son	Twelfth Night
Gulliver's Travels	1984	Uncle Tom's Cabin
Hamlet	The Odyssey	Waiting for Godot
Hard Times	Oedipus Trilogy	Wuthering Heights

RESEARCH & EDUCATION ASSOCIATION
61 Ethel Road W. • Piscataway, New Jersey 08854
Phone: (908) 819-8880

Please send me more information about MAXnotes®.

Name _____

Address _____

City _____ State _____ Zip _____

SSD
Bradfield College

James Joyce's

Dubliners

Text by
Gina Taglieri
(M.A. Columbia University)
English Department
Fashion Institute of Technology
State University of New York
New York, New York

Illustrations by
Bob Rodefeld

Research & Education Association

SSD
Bradfield College

MAXnotes® for
DUBLINERS

Copyright © 1996 by Research & Education
Association. All rights reserved. No part of this
book may be reproduced in any form without
permission of the publisher.

Printed in the United States of America

Library of Congress Catalog Card Number 96-67454

International Standard Book Number 0-87891-011-5

MAXnotes® is a registered trademark of
Research & Education Association, Piscataway, New Jersey 08854